Damocles On The Couch

How Simple Logic And Humorous Stories Can Lead Us To Healthy Living

Herbert L. Stricklin

Order this book online at www.trafford.com
or email orders@trafford.com

Most Trafford titles are also available at major online book retailers.

Printed in the United States of America.

ISBN: 978-1-4669-7299-5 (sc)
ISBN: 978-1-4669-7300-8 (e)

Trafford rev. 12/27/2012

 www.trafford.com

North America & international
toll-free: 1 888 232 4444 (USA & Canada)
phone: 250 383 6864 ♦ fax: 812 355 4082

Contents

Preface

At the time that this book was penned (or word processed) I find myself at the ripe old age of 47. To be honest, it is difficult for me to conceptualize that number because for so many years that was how old my friend's parents were. It is also difficult to wrap my head around the idea that I have been a counseling professional for 23 years. However, as I consult the calendar I see that it is the case. For almost a quarter of a century, I have worked with individuals who are facing the darkest times in their lives. As daunting a task as it can be, I truly count myself as living a very blessed life. For as pained and injured as individuals are when I first meet them in my office, I have the distinct privilege to witness them access their natural born courage to take on and slay the emotional dragons they face in their lives. Of course not every story has a happy ending, but I have truly witnessed my share of profound transformations.

The actual writing of this book has taken close to two years. That is not two years of straight devotion to the book, as I have also maintained a full-time private practice and a near full-time teaching load, but it has taken much more time to complete than I originally expected. In reality, this book began much more than two years ago. It actually predates my entering the counseling profession. It began prior to my entering graduate school at Benedictine University, and even before my undergraduate time at Loyola University of Chicago. It even begins prior to my high school and grammar school days in Lockport, IL. This book actually began with the beginning of me.

You see counseling is a human relationship. There is no way that it can be done effectively any other way. In my opinion, a skilled counselor takes their own life experiences and who they are as an individual, blends them with the theories and techniques that they learn, and creates a therapeutic milieu in which the client can examine their lives and concerns, making changes as necessary. Therefore, my path to becoming a counselor began with my becoming who I am as an individual. It is the sum total of my life experiences, the people I have met, the challenges that I have faced, my successes and failures, the people who have taught me (both formally and informally), the tears that I have cried, and the laughs that I have shared. My spiritual life and relationship with God are at the core of who I am, and ultimately the clinician that I am.

Working with clients, I try to share with them a model of life that is fairly simple. I often relate these principles through stories that I tell. I find this method to be highly effective since it requires the person hearing the story to identify the meaning as it relates to them. This communicates the meaning on a much deeper level than simply relaying theories and facts that go in one ear and out the other. Within the pages of this book are many stories that I have shared with individuals that I have worked with through the years. Some are humorous, others are not, but they all carry a message. It is my hope that as you read through this work that you will find it interesting, thought provoking, and maybe even entertaining at times. Writing this book was truly a labor of love, and I appreciate in advance your taking the time to share in my words.

1

It's Ok To Be A Crab

lright, I have to admit that the heading of this section is a bit misleading, but it is a great lead-in to a simple bit of logic that we can learn from a common crustacean, the hermit crab. You see, nature has much to offer us in regards to lessons for healthy living. Now I am not in any way an expert in the field of animal sciences (although I was a biology major for a year and a half in college), but I do know the basics of a hermit crab. You see a hermit crab lives in a shell, but it is not of its own creation. The hermit crab finds an abandoned shell, moves in, and makes it his/her home. That shell performs several important functions for the hermit crab, not the least of which is security. When the hermit crab feels threatened it pulls inside of the shell to hide out from potential predators.

Sounds like a pretty simple plan, but there is a catch. The hermit crab, being a living organism, continues to grow inside of this shell until one day it faces a dilemma. The shell that affords it safety and security no longer fits. What is the crab to do? The crab really has two options at this point: 1) Stay in the cramped and dysfunctional shell and be safe; or 2) Leave the security of the shell, and make itself vulnerable for a period of time so it can venture out in search of a larger shell that will allow it room to grow. At this point, I probably don't have to tell you that the hermit crab always chooses growth over safety.

That is because that is what living things are designed to do, to live and grow. Frequently in life we face the same dilemma as the hermit crab. Not that we have to fear being eaten by a bass, but we do have to leave our familiar "shells" to afford ourselves the opportunity to grow. Many individuals who are change-averse will scratch and claw to stay hold-up in their cramped and dysfunctional shells, but when they do this they are battling against their basic design. As the saying goes, "In life, change is inevitable, growth is optional."

Now let me clarify something. I am not suggesting that we run helter-skelter through life following every whim that happens by. That would be silly, and quite often dangerous. The hermit crab doesn't just abandon shell at the first twinge of discomfort. It explores the environment, carefully searching out a shell that will provide for its needs and will allow it room to grow. In similar fashion, we need to stay in tune with our lives. We need to identify sources of discomfort and determine whether it is a passing occurrence like a case of the "Mondays" or something deep inside prompting us to change or grow in some way.

I want to talk for a minute about discomfort. Most people errantly believe that discomfort is a bad thing. Actually, the opposite is true in most cases. Eat some tainted food, and the GI discomfort helps you to get rid of what is potentially poisoning you. Get a cold, and the fever helps kill the bug while the cough helps to clear your lungs. Step on something sharp, and the pain in your foot gets you to move off of it. You get the picture. Most people, however, view emotional discomfort as something to avoid or escape as quickly as possible. I am here to tell you that if this describes you, you are missing some prime opportunities to grow. Take for example, your boss has a talk with you about the decline in the quality of your work. You could just leave with your tail between your legs and go complain to co-workers about what an ogre you work for. Opportunity lost. You go on a series of bad dates and you say to friends, "Man, there just aren't any good men/women left anymore." Well, that might be, or maybe you are not quite handling these dates very well yourself. You take a test and get a "D". Maybe the professor is a jerk, and has it out for you. Or maybe going to a party the night before a test wasn't quite a wise choice.

Now that does not mean that all misfortune is of our own doing, but we do have to sort through these situations with a critical eye and take accountability when it is called for. There are times in life when we lose, and that is not a bad thing either, unless you respond to it by quitting, then its "game over". If we take our defeats and learn from them, and the discomfort associated with them, we can improve ourselves and grow.

Many parents these days are unwittingly guilty of this very thing while raising their children. The "politically correct" view that "everyone wins" and "no one loses" is total garbage. I am reminded of the story of a woman who was walking through the woods when she came upon a baby bunny in front of her on the path she was walking. Fearing that the defenseless bunny would not be able to care for itself, she scooped it up, took it home, and placed it inside of a chicken wire fence. She fed it scraps from her garden each day, and even brought it inside when the nights were too cold. Well, that rabbit grew quite large with the endless buffet that it was provided. One day, feeling confident that the rabbit was large enough to fend for itself, the woman took the rabbit back to the woods to release it back into the wild. She took the rabbit to the precise place on the trail that she found him several months earlier. She tearfully kissed the rabbit on the head, placed him on the ground, and walked back to her car. The rabbit realized that it was kind of hungry, but its food dish was nowhere in sight. He hopped into a clearing because it was easier to get a look around there. Just as the woman reached her car, the rabbit turned to see her drive off, and was promptly eaten by a fox (bet ya didn't see that one coming). The moral of the story is, let your children learn from their mistakes and defeats or they will all be hopelessly devoured by predatory animals. Actually, what can be learned from this story is that the lessons that we encounter through the struggles that we face in life help to prepare us for the challenges that we will eventually have to face on our own. The famous analyst, Dr. Alfred Adler boldly stated that when we pamper a child (do for them what they can or should be able to do for themselves) we actually are contributing to handicapping the child. Pampering, to Adler, is one of the worst forms of child abuse because it fosters the belief that the child is incapable of doing for themselves, and that others will always do for them.

So let's say that you are in a place where you are tired of making excuses and avoiding the discomfort that is urging you to grow. How does one go about the process of constructing a meaningful life? After all, if you are going to work through this process you want to make sure that you do it in a healthy and a lasting way. The pages to follow will include many of the suggestions that I make to the people with whom I work when they are preparing to undertake this process.

The first thing I encourage people to incorporate in their plan is patience. I have to admit that throughout a large portion of my life patience has not been one of my virtues. This was made glaringly obvious to me by my son, Jonathon, one night when I was trying to get him into bed. It was shortly after Christmas and Jonathon was busy playing with his new-found treasures from the holiday. I was busy trying to get everything done that I needed to do to get to bed, and one of the items on the agenda was getting Jonathon to brush his teeth. After numerous prompts for him to do this, he comes out of his room to show me a toy he is playing with. This is not consistent with brushing teeth so I ignore his attempt to show me his toy and respond instead with, "Brush your teeth". Not to be detoured, he again attempts to show me his toy. Now my parental glue begins to give way and I say to him in one of my less than shining moments as a parent, "Brush your teeth, brush your teeth, brush your teeth!" He gently looks up at me in my full jerkdom and says, "Dad, I am a little guy. I can only do one thing at a time." Lesson learned, score one for the kids.

I was working with a client who was firmly entrenched in his belief that things were about as good as they were going to get for him, and the thought of change in his life was fear-provoking. During one particular session the light bulb went off and he realized that things could get better and he wanted the change right now. I pointed out that he had lived his life a certain way for a long period of time, and it is not realistic to think that lasting change is going to come out of an impulsive, poorly thought out plan. As the saying goes, evolution lasts longer than revolution. Still he wanted to know what he needed to do to get his life turned around and quick! To put it into perspective for him, I asked him this question, "Have you ever baked a cake?" He responded that he had, and then I asked him how long it took and at what temperature. He stated that he thought it was around 350 degrees for 30 minutes or so. I then asked him how the cake would turn out if he tried to bake it in 15 minutes at 700 degrees. With life changes, faster does not necessarily mean better.

When preparing to make changes in one's life, it also not time to drag things out and to have the plan take forever. Conversely, a person must have a sense of urgency in their plan. Again, that does not mean to hurry through the process, but rather to prioritize the changes that must be made and to roll up the sleeves and get to work.

2
Who Is In Charge Here?

L et's face it, control (or a lack thereof) is a huge issue in people's lives these days. Life is moving so fast that it seems that we require the Vulcan death-grip just to hang on. Many people who make their way to my office arrive for the first session looking as if they are returning from the front lines of some major battle, and in many ways they are. They are trying to meet deadlines, care for children, care for elderly parents, pay the bills, mow the grass, cook meals, do the laundry, answer emails, attend the church meeting, return the call to their friend who called last week, and if possible send a text to their spouse to see if they can find 15 minutes of quality time sometime next week. Sound familiar? Unfortunately, for most of us it does. The world is a demanding place, and how you approach those demands can make all the difference in determining if you are one of the survivors, or if you are a casualty of life.

Because of the frequency of this problem, there is a subject that I almost always cover during my first session with a new client. The concept I present to them does not lessen the demands they face, but it does help them to have a puncher's chance at surviving the rat race they find themselves in. The theory is known as "Locus of Control", or in English, where is the control located. The original architect of this theory was Julian B. Rotter, who described individual differences in people who attribute the reasons that things happen in their life as being caused by either internal sources (their own behavior) or external sources (other's behavior). You see all of us have an internal and an external locus of control. Internal locus of control includes all of the things in this world that we can control, and without oversimplifying things, there are only three things that are under our control. We can control our thoughts, our feelings, and our behavior. Now that may not sound like much, but believe me, on most days managing those three things in a healthy way is a full-time job in itself. Everything else falls into the category of external locus of control. This limitless list may include things such as the traffic jam you find yourself in coming home from work, the tantrum your two year old chooses to throw in the checkout isle at the grocery store, or your mechanic who says that the work needed on your car is "a little more extensive" than was first thought. Again, the people who I see in counseling all have problems such as these, but they also have some that are more grueling with which to deal. They have a cancer that was just diagnosed, a spouse of twenty-plus years who "loves them, but is not sure if they are in-love with them", a boss who thanks them for fifteen years of dedicated service but their position is being down-sized, or a child who has been through several treatment programs but continues to use drugs. Yes, the world does happen.

When it comes to the matter of internal locus of control (our thoughts, our feelings, and our behavior), one of these elements, our thoughts, takes precedence over the other two. The reason for this is simple. Our thoughts always precede our behavior. Now many of us have heard people say that they acted impulsively or the "didn't even think before they acted", but this just isn't true. Now they may not have gone through a very thorough thought process or their thinking may have been hurried or flawed, but they did "think" before they "acted". When it comes to the relationship between thoughts and feelings, it is very similar to that between thoughts and behavior. Feelings exist as trailers to thought. Therefore how you think about things will determine what emotion is present. This is a particularly challenging problem for people who have the tendency of personalizing matters. If they think that others are directing their actions specifically at them, they are predisposed to hurts and slights that are not really meant to be there.

Since the relationship between thoughts and feelings is so important, and can make all the difference in a person's emotional well-being, I want to offer an example of how our thoughts about a particular incident can effectively change our emotional response based on how we think about it. Imagine that you are at work and you are walking down the hallway. Approaching you is a coworker that we'll call Bob. As Bob approaches you, you offer a greeting, "Good morning, Bob" to which Bob does not respond. We start thinking to ourselves, "Well, that pretty good. What is his problem? What a jerk." So now we are miffed with Bob for a good part of the day until we learn later that Bob actually has a sick child at home. He was not being rude to us at all; he is just preoccupied with his concern for his child. Now the emotion that we experience is compassion rather than anger. Nothing changed in regards to the initial incident with passing Bob in the hallway, other than how we think about it, and we have a completely different emotional experience.

To get back to the idea of locus of control, and how it can help someone deal with these concerns, let's take a look at some examples.

Example 1: Diagnosis

You schedule an appointment to go see your doctor because you are feeling fatigued. You are pretty sure it's nothing because you take good care of yourself by exercising and trying to eat right. It's probably just the extra stress at the office as deadlines are looming. You are figuring he will give you a B-12 shot, tell you to take a vacation, and send you on your way. A few days later, the test results come back and he says he needs you to come into the office to discuss them. You sit down in his office and for the first time you are concerned because his usual upbeat demeanor is replaced by something much more serious. Then he tells you that you have leukemia. For a moment it's as if the world stops. Time seems frozen, but a million thoughts run through you head. Once it sinks in, what do you do?

Elizabeth Kubler-Ross, in her well-known book, <u>On Death And Dying</u>, talks about the five stages of grief. The stages, as she describes are *denial, anger, bargaining, depression, and acceptance.* These are normal, and in many ways healthy stages of grief, but I want to focus on healthy vs unhealthy ways of dealing with this situation. First we'll explore the unhealthy. You get stuck in one of the stages such as denial, anger, or depression. This leads to you behavioral response. You either go on with things, acting as if nothing is wrong, or you plop down, emotionally defeated, arms crossed, so angry that you could scream, but you do nothing. This is the worst thing that you could do, nothing.

Now let's take a look at the healthy approach to this same matter. You will go through the same stages of grief, but you don't allow yourself to become mired in any one of them. You must assess the things that you can control and the things that you cannot. First of all, you cannot control that you have leukemia. That you must accept. You also cannot control how far your condition has advanced to the point of your diagnosis. You can't control the extent of medical research on your condition as well as the treatments that are available to you. Now let's take a look at what you can control (thoughts, feelings, and behavior). You can maintain thoughts such as "I am going to fight this thing with all that I have", "I am going to study this condition to learn all that there is to know about it (knowledge is power)", "I am going to find doctors who specialize in this condition, and I am going to get them working on me", and "I am not going down without a hell of a fight". Maintaining thoughts like this will result in the emotions of hope, encouragement, determination, and optimism, all of which are essential to have in your arsenal if you are taking on a disease like cancer. Behaviorally, you have to back up your thoughts and feelings with actions. The things that you tell yourself need to be brought to fruition. Do not give up. Exhaust every option, and keep fighting the fight until it is clear that there is nothing else to be done. This is the sentiment expressed in the poem by Dylan Thomas, "Do not go gentle into that good night". Every living thing has an inherent will to live. You know this if you have ever tried to eradicate weeds from the cracks in your sidewalk. No matter how many times you spray them with herbicide, they will keep coming back. We have to make sure that we demonstrate that same determination.

Example 2: Relationship

You have been married many years, and like every relationship, you have had your share of ups-and-downs. Lately you have been on one of the downward spirals. You don't think much of it since you and your spouse have gotten out of troubled spots in your relationship before. You get home from work on Friday and your spouse greets you as you enter your home with, "We need to talk". They go on to tell you that they have not been happy in a long time. "It's not you", they go on to say, and "they love you, but they are not *in love with you*". They say that they have given this a lot of thought and they think it would be best for you to separate for a while so you can figure out what the two of you should do. What do you do?

Getting hit with devastating news like that can send a person into a tailspin. Often individuals will allow their hurt and anger to get the best of them. They will beg and plead with their partner, they will try to guilt them into not leaving, or they will tell the other "don't let the door hit ya on the way out!" Certainly a case could be made for any of these responses, but none of them will work if you have any desire to save your marriage. Begging and pleading shows no self-respect. Why would someone who has stated their desire to leave be swayed by your groveling? Guilt doesn't work because it only stirs more negative feelings and defensiveness. "You know, honey, I was all set to leave, but now that you have helped me to feel really bad about myself, I am all excited to make this thing work!" And showing them the door will accelerate the process of ending the marriage, so if you have any hope to salvage this thing, curb your anger. I am not saying that you should not be angry. Certainly, that will be one of a myriad of emotions that you will experience. Just be careful what you do with it, and how you express it.

So what is the healthy way of dealing with this situation if your desire is to try to save the relationship? Let's sort out what you can and can't control. Well, you can't control how your spouse feels. Trying to talk them out of how they feel will often only entrench them more in their decision. You can't control whether they stay or not. It may make no sense at all to you why they would want to leave your home, but taking them hostage is not an option. You also cannot control the reaction of family and friends as they find out about the developments in your relationship. Finally, you cannot control whether the other person legally files for divorce. Sure you can throw up legal roadblocks, but often you are delaying the inevitable. If this happens to you, make sure that you defend yourself with qualified legal counsel, but don't fight the person, thinking that if you make it difficult enough they will give in and come back to you.

I tell people who are in this situation that it is very important to make certain decisions early in the process. They have to do some real soul searching and decide how they are going to conduct themselves through this process. Let's go to our thoughts, feelings, and behaviors. You have to decide whether you want to fight for your relationship, understanding that this will require a great expenditure of energy with no guarantee of return. I also encourage people to honestly assess the way that they have functioned in this relationship. This does not mean that they are to bare the brunt of the relationship problems, and assume responsibility for things that they did not do. You do have to be mature enough to accept responsibility for some poor behavior that you have demonstrated in the relationship, as well as some of the opportunities missed to care for and to maintain the relationship. If the relationship is to have any chance, both of you will have to do this work, but for right now you can only control your portion. As for feelings, you better wear a seat belt! You will experience a whole host of feelings going through this process. You will feel hurt, sadness, anger, confusion, disbelief, regret, frustration, and quite possibly depression to name just a few. Again, you are entitled to these emotions, but they do not give you license to unleash your wrath on the other. That is not going to improve the odds of repairing the damage to your relationship. Finally, there is your behavior. Conduct yourself in a respectful way. Avoid getting into mud-slinging contests. If the other person is being disrespectful or rude, ask them to stop. If they don't, end the conversation stating that, "I am open to talking to you, but I will not be spoken to in this way". End of story. I also encourage people to communicate their intentions to their spouse. An example of this is as follows, "This divorce is not something that I want. However, I understand that you have the right to end the marriage if that is what you really want. I am not going to stand in your way, but I am going to protect myself in whatever way I need to during this process. If you ever have a desire to stop the divorce and work on our marriage again, please let me know. I am willing to do my part to make it work." Now here is the thing I have to tell people in this situation. You only have to tell the other person this once. Unless they have suffered a significant head injury and they live their life fifteen minutes at a time, they can remember what you have said. Telling them over and over will be experienced by them as being controlling . . . . because that is what it is.

If you find (or have found) yourself in this situation, I want to express my sympathy, as well as my encouragement. Fighting for your relationship is one of the most daunting tasks that a person will ever experience, especially if you are doing it unilaterally. In our "microwave society" there is a sense that it is easier to throw out something that is not working and replace it with something new. When it comes to relationships, unless there is something abusive or harmful going on, most people who choose to do the work to repair what is broken in their current relationship are happy that they did so in the end. It is truly one of the joys that I experience in my professional life when a marriage on the brink of divorce is reclaimed.

Example 3: Unemployment

In these days of economic plight, this is an all-too-often experienced problem for people. They work hard for their employer, coming in on weekends, starting early and staying late, taking work home with them, and the sum result is their job is gone in an instant. Quite often this occurs in a very un-ceremonial fashion, with the person being escorted to the door without the opportunity to return to clean out their belongings or to say farewell to co-workers. All of a sudden the bills that seemed challenging with a job are horrifying with no real source of income. Your pride is damaged, your identity is crumbling, your future is in doubt and it's not even 10AM.

Sometimes the cavalcade of emotions resulting from this experience will lead people to refer to this situation as being "overwhelming". Whenever I hear this word used in a situation such as this, I am compelled to challenge the person's use of it. It's not that I am trying to diminish the significance of what it is that they are going through, but remember the relationship between thoughts and feelings. Whatever thought you entertain in your mind will determine the emotional experience that you have. Loosely described, the word overwhelmed means that the person's ability to cope is exceeded by the circumstances that they are facing. When people encounter problems such as job loss, house in foreclosure, or bankruptcy they are facing problems that are much more than they would want to be facing, not much more than they are capable of facing.

Unhealthy ways of dealing with this situation would be to stew in the unfair nature of the situation. You allow the bitterness and anger to take hold, eroding you emotionally from the inside out. This in no way helps you to get your life back on track. To go out and decry how wrong the company was to treat you the way that they did, helps no one. Maybe after weeks or even months of sending out resumes with barely a sniff of an offer you are tempted to give up, throw up your hands in defeat. Let me tell you that this kind of thinking is your worst enemy in times like these, and you do not have the "luxury" of entertaining such ideas. Pessimism will destroy you at this point, leading you to inactivity and ultimate defeat.

The healthy way to approach a problem such as this would have us looking at what we can control and what we can't. We can't control the fact that our employer gave us the shaft. We also can't control that the job market is thin, nor can we control the fact the economy is on life support. What can we control? You guessed it-our thoughts, our feelings, and our behavior. Again, that may not sound like much, but it is really quite a bit when you think about it. You must maintain optimistic thoughts. You can get through this, you have always figured things out in the past. This is something that most people do not give themselves credit for. If you are still alive and drawing breath, which I hope most people reading this book are, then you can say with total confidence that you have never faced anything that you have not been able to deal with. Now if you are like most people, that doesn't mean that you have handled everything in a totally healthy way, but some way or another you got yourself through it. With that in mind, the only question left to answer regarding your current problems are how well you will handle them and how soon you will handle them. Maintaining optimistic thoughts will allow you to access your courage. This is an essential element in facing difficult problems in life. Alfred Adler, the famous psychoanalyst from the early 1900's would often say that people in need of counseling are people who are discouraged. Now think of that word. It literally means to "disconnect from your courage", to dis-courage. Adler also said that an important role for the therapist is to encourage the client. In other words, the therapist must help them to re-connect with their courage. Maintaining hope and accessing your courage will help you to stay determined. You keep working at it until you achieve your goal.

A story that I like to tell when it comes to optimism and pessimism really brings this to light. There was a father who had twin sons. He loved them both, but the sons could not be more different in their personalities. One son was an eternal pessimist, and the other was an eternal optimist. The father's concern was that neither of these extremes was going to be effective in dealing with the life ahead of them. The pessimist would never experience true enjoyment in life, and the optimist would be faced with constant disappointment. So the father developed a plan to address this situation. Their birthdays were approaching, so he was going to purchase lavish gifts for the pessimist so that he could see the good in the world and for the optimist there would be a box with a shovel full of horse manure to bring him back to earth. Their birthday arrived and the pessimist sat down in front of a huge stack of gifts, and the optimist sat there with one. The pessimist went first. He opened the first gift, which was a toy, and stated boldly that it would probably break soon and he would not be able to play with it after that. The nice clothes that he opened were tossed to the side with comments such as, "I will outgrow this soon" or "This material will stain and rip easily". The father is decimated, for soon he will have two depressed children, once the box of manure is opened. Well, the pessimist opens the last gift detailing all its flaws and short-comings, and then attention switches to the optimist, who has been patiently waiting with his one gift. The father cringes as the optimist tears off the ribbon, lifts off the lid, looks inside, and yells .... "Yippee!" The astonished father looks on with disbelief and states, "Yippee? All you got was a box of horse crap!" His son exclaimed back, "I know! That means there is a pony around here somewhere!" Now that is optimism.

Example 4: Child On Drugs

Your teenage son, whom you love very much, has gone astray. Some years back he started hanging with a different crowd of kids. The way he dressed changed, his grades dropped, behavior problems started popping up at school, and he became increasingly disrespectful towards you and your spouse. He just seemed angry all the time. He started sneaking out of the house at night, and in general became much more secretive. You had suspicions, but it couldn't be . . . he was just going through a stage. Then things started disappearing from the house. You started questioning how much money you carried in your wallet. Then jewelry and video games started to come up missing. You ask, but he always denies. Usually he has a pretty convincing story to back it up. Then the call from the police station comes. He was caught trying to sell drugs to an undercover police officer. What do you do?

The unhealthy response is to listen to his explanations that he was "set up" or "it was the first time he had ever done this sort of thing". Do not allow the fact that you do not want to think of your child as having a drug problem to cloud your judgment. This is not a time when denial should be allowed to enter the scene. Avoid becoming an enabler of this problem. Do not look the other way. Do not settle for empty promises of never doing this again. People with drug and alcohol problems can be very convincing, especially when it involves parents who cannot stand to think of their child having this sort of problem. If you are not part of the solution, you are part of the problem.

The healthy response to such a problem again begins with sorting out what you can control and what you cannot. You cannot control your teenager's behavior, but you can control the consequences to it. You can get them into treatment, but you cannot make them make use of it. And in some cases you must make some very difficult decisions. You may have to tell the child that if they continue to use drugs, and they are older than 18, that they cannot live in your home. I have heard many a heart-wrenching tale of parents emotionally devastated by their child's drug use. These stories come from all races and all backgrounds. In managing your thoughts, you must be determined to be consistent with what is acceptable and what is not acceptable. You must understand that you will feel some painful emotions through this process, but you cannot allow them to cloud your judgment. And probably the most important element of dealing with this kind of problem is to be consistent. If you say something, mean it. Do not say something that you do not intend to back up with action. If you need support in going through something like this, search out a local Al-Anon group to meet with other parents and families dealing with drug-addicted family members.

The point of this discussion, and of these examples, is to help you to walk through some very difficult life problems contrasting healthy vs unhealthy responses. When things are going well in life we can often get by without being as intensely vigilant of locus of control issues. However, when the trials come, and they will come, you have to be prepared. You have to approach these problems (and others like them) in a way that maximizes your chances for success. Separate the things that you can control vs the things that you cannot, and then focus your energy on the things that you can. The things that you cannot control will require you to "let it go", or at the very least, find a healthy way to cope with them.

One final note on healthy approaches to dealing with problems, involves a basic fact as to how our minds function. We don't often think about it, but our minds are incapable of thinking in the negative. Let me give you an example. Try to *not* think of a white bear. Really try . . . . don't think of a white bear. The reality is that when we try to *not* think about something, we think about it all the more. We are much better off telling ourselves what we are going to do about the problem that we are facing. Ask an alcoholic what they plan to do about their problem drinking and they say, "I am just going to not drink". Really . . . . and to think I spent all those years in college and graduate school, and it is as simple as that! The truth is that it isn't. The person's plan should be to get with a qualified professional to help them with their treatment. They should learn what purpose drinking serves for them (to escape, to deal with anxiety, to deal with boredom or loneliness, etc.). They should develop a plan to address that issue in a healthy way. They should make themselves accountable to someone who will hold them to what they say. Also, you should have a Plan B, and a Plan C, and enough "Plans" to implement until you can master your problem. And make sure that you are controlling your thoughts, your feelings, and your behavior.

3

Ya Gotta Believe!

Mike Ditka, the Hall of Fame tight end and Superbowl winning head coach for the Chicago Bears is much better at football than singing. This was proven some years back when he was supposed to sing "Take Me Out To The Ballgame" during the seventh inning stretch for the Chicago Cubs at Wrigley Field. Well, on this particular day, Iron Mike was running a bit late, and club executives were scrambling, trying to figure out how to replace him. Just at the last minute, his limo arrived, and he ran up the walkway to get to the TV booth to sing the song. Out of breath from his upward climb, he sang the song so quickly that the poor organist hadn't a chance to keep up with him. At the end of the song he screams out to the crowd and to the Cubs team, who of course are losing (I can say this, being a life-long Cubs fan), "Ya gotta believe! Let's go!". Unwittingly, Mike Ditka passed along some very important advice to all of us about the power of our thoughts.

You see, all too often in life people develop or adopt beliefs about themselves that are just not true. Many theorists in psychology have incorporated the importance of beliefs into their theories of personality. Alfred Adler, a contemporary of Sigmund Freud, talked about the power of *guiding principles* and *private logic*, and the role they play in determining patterns of behavior. Albert Ellis, the Psychologist behind the theory of Rational Emotive Therapy, would often speak of the *ABC's* of mental health. In this model, the "A" stood for *Activating Event* (a life event that the person encountered), the "B" stood for the *Belief* about the event (this could be either a rational belief or an irrational belief), and the "C" stood for the *Consequence* (or the feeling that resulted from the pairing of the event and the belief). The theory points out that these interactions between events, beliefs, and the resulting feelings happen continuously throughout our day. Sometimes we are conscious of them and sometimes we are not, but either way, we still feel the resulting emotions.

Sometimes the beliefs are rational beliefs, and in those cases the feeling that should occur does occur. Other times, however, the thoughts are false or irrational in nature, and the resulting feeling is inappropriate for the situation. Let's look at a couple of examples. Imagine a child is experiencing the painful life event of having a pet put to sleep. This would be the *activating event.* The child is dealing with the thoughts of not having her pet, and is remembering all of the fun times that she had with her pet and she is missing him. These would be the *beliefs* that are associated with this event. In response to this she is feeling the *emotional consequence* of feeling sad. She is feeling sad because that is what people feel when they experience a loss. A second example might be a guy who has not gotten opportunities to advance at work (*activating event*). He believes his employer just doesn't like him and they are being unfair *(belief)*. In regards to this set of circumstances, he is feeling angry *(emotional consequence)*. But when we take a closer look at the realities of this situation we see that this man's belief is not entirely reality based. He often comes to work late, does sub-standard work, and has been caught more than once watching episodes of *House* on his computer during work time. Therefore, his feelings of anger towards his employer are unfounded. He would be better served to be disappointed in his lack of effort on the job. The discomfort of this disappointment might just be enough to get him to put forth a solid effort, improving his chances for a promotion.

My favorite story regarding the relationship between beliefs and emotions comes from a seminar that I attended many years back. The speaker was describing a time when he was visiting a friend in the western part of the country, and they were rock climbing. The speaker said that he was the lead climber on this day, and they were well up the side of a cliff when he reached up to a ledge to pull himself up and he heard a rattling sound. At that moment he became intimately familiar with the relationship between thoughts and feelings. His perceptions told him the sound was a snake, his feeling was terror, and his behavioral response was to freeze on the side of that rock. After a couple of seconds he looked down to his friend for help and he saw his friend standing on a ledge beneath him shaking a little tin of beans. Yeah, a little humor there on the side of the cliff. Well, I am not sure of the content of the conversation between the speaker and his rock climbing friend following that, but the point is that he believed the sound to be a snake, and the emotions that he experienced were just as real as if it were a snake.

These examples that I have given relate to specific incidents that people could potentially experience, but the possible harmful effects can go far beyond this. Maintaining unrealistic, irrational, or otherwise toxic thoughts about ourselves and the world around us can have a crippling effect on our lives. Most personality theorists believe that the core of our personalities (our beliefs about ourselves, men, women, and the world in general) is set by the age of five or six. From that point on, we maintain these same beliefs, modifying them slightly as we go. As we have been discussing, these beliefs will directly relate to the feelings that we have in life, the behaviors we engage in, and the decisions that we make. If these thoughts are unhealthy, they can permeate our lives having potentially catastrophic effects.

The common flea is a tiny creature, but it has a tremendous ability to jump. Comparatively it would be like a human jumping over a tall building with a single bound. Research has shown, however, that if you take fleas and put them into a jar with a lid on it the fleas will eventually adjust their jumping height to just barely miss hitting their heads on the lid. If you allow them to condition themselves to these circumstances for a period of time you can actually remove the lid and the fleas won't escape. They still believe that it is not in their best interest to jump any higher and hit the lid so they remain confined even though freedom is just a centimeter or two away. How many lives have been stunted, and how many dreams have gone unrealized by toxic thinking just like this?

All too often I work with clients who hold these same debilitating beliefs about themselves. "I'm not good enough, so I won't try out for the team." "I can't do math, so I won't even study for the test." "I could never do that job, someone else is probably more qualified." "I know she would never go out with me, so why do I want to embarrass myself by getting turned down?" "I could never give a speech in front of that many people." "I could never write a book that people would be interested in reading (hmmm . . . sounds familiar)." "I am a loser, and I will never amount to anything." All of these statements are things that I have heard from clients and friends, and some I have uttered myself previously in life. The one thing they all have in common is that they are untrue, or at the very least, they are unproven.

The Wizard of Oz is a movie that makes this very point (although to this day I have a hard time watching it because those flying monkeys creep me out). In the movie, Dorothy, the Tin Man, The Cowardly Lion, and The Scarecrow all make their way down the yellow brick road to see the Wizard. They believe that he possesses special powers that will help them to fill in their lives with what is missing. Once they make it to the Wizard, and realize that even though he wants to be viewed as the all-powerful Wizard, he is really just a short, dumpy guy (a great example for understanding the Narcissistic Personality). Even though they are initially disappointed to find this out, the Wizard is still able to provide them with the answer to their problems. He informs them that what they came to him to find, they really had all along. They just did not believe in themselves.

Martin Seligman, the director of the Positive Psychology Center is famous for exploring the phenomenon of "Learned Helplessness". This theory describes how animals and humans can continue to behave in a helpless fashion even after opportunities to escape painful circumstances are made available to them again. Here is a brief synopsis of the experiment that led to this theory. A dog is fitted with a shock collar (back off PETA) and then placed in a room that has half of the floor tiled in all white and half of the room tiled in a black and white checker pattern. Phase one of the experiment involves the dog receiving electric shocks whenever he is standing on the all-white part of the floor. The dogs response is to move around until he realizes that the shocks stop in the checkered area, and then he stays on that side of the room. Phase II involves the dog getting shocked whenever it is on the checkered side, so after moving around the room, he settles on the all-white tile. Phase III sees the dog being randomly shocked no matter where he is in the room. He moves around frantically trying to figure out what he can do to make the painful stimulus go away. After a period of unsuccessful trials, the dog slumps to the floor and just trembles. Phase IV of the experiment sees the conditions return to what they were in stage one, the dog is shocked whenever he is on the white side and he can escape the shock by moving to the checkered side. Nonetheless, the dog continues to lie there trembling, unwilling to figure out how to escape the pain. Many people who make their way to my office are dealing with very similar issues. Not that someone has fitted them with a shock collar, but life has in some way "zapped" them and they feel helpless to do anything about this.

This is what happens to the student who tries, but "just can't get it", or the unemployed person who has stopped sending resumes because it is "pointless", or the lonely person who just stays sequestered in their home because "the right person is just not out there". I truly believe that the misapplication of the word *can't* is one of the most debilitating things that people do to themselves. They say that they can't do this or they can't do that, when what they really mean is that they haven't been able to or they haven't tried at all. This is a very important distinction because, as we have already learned, our thoughts are precursors to our feelings. "Can't" is an endpoint, something that has no chance of happening, "haven't been able to" means that you just haven't found the right formula yet. To show how our thoughts and perceptions affect our experience of things, I want you to take a moment to examine the figure on the next page:

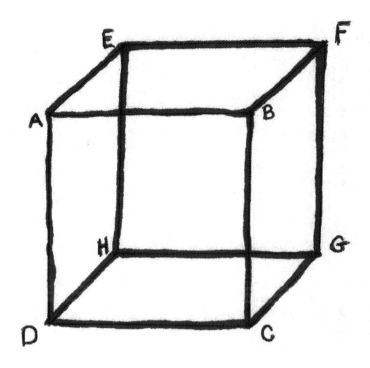

Look at the figure so that you see the ABCD side facing towards you. It may take a minute, but eventually it will come to you. Once you get that, change your perception so that you see the EFGH side coming out towards you. This is usually a bit more challenging, but if you keep working at it, you should get it. The experience that people have when they do this exercise is for it to seem as if the object shifted. In actuality, the object didn't move an inch. The different way that you looked at it gave you a different experience of the cube. Now this is just a simple example of changing perceptions. Imagine what things would be like if you could take many of those "can't" beliefs that have taken up residence in your life and turn them into "why not?" beliefs.

One final set of cognitive distortions (errant beliefs) that will frequently get people into bad places emotionally is often referred to as "all-or-nothing thinking". This concept was developed by Aaron Beck, the creator of the *Beck Depression Inventory* and *the Beck Anxiety Inventory.* Beck believes that "all-or-nothing thinking" is one of the key contributors to depression. Here are some common examples of "all-or-nothing thinking": "No one likes me", "Everyone is against me", "Things never go right for me", "The deck is always stacked against me." Well, if these statements were accurate reflections of a person's world, they would be perfectly entitled to be depressed, but they are, in fact, not accurate. What the person using phrases such as these actually should be saying is "Not as many people like me as I would like" or "Things don't go the way I want them to as much as I would like". Now these may still not be exactly positive ways of thinking, but remember that the feelings associated with the thoughts you entertain don't edit your thoughts. If you tell yourself that no one likes you, the feeling that you experience will be despair and/or loneliness. Change your thoughts on this to something along the lines of, "I don't have as many friends as I would like. I need to get out there and work on that" and the feelings will be more hopeful and optimistic. Now I am not suggesting just slapping on the rose-colored glasses and everything will be perfect in you world, but which of those ways of looking at things is more based in reality? And which of those ways of looking at things will help to keep you out of learned helplessness?

One final word on the power of thoughts in healthy living comes from the life of Thomas Edison. The story is told that prior to his successfully creating the incandescent light bulb; Edison was being interviewed by a reporter. The reporter bluntly asked him, "Mr. Edison, isn't it frustrating that you have tried thousands of ways to make a light bulb and you haven't learned anything?" Edison boldly looked back at the reporter and stated, "Actually, my good man, I have learned many things. I have learned thousands of ways *not* to make a light bulb!" That, my dear friends, is the best antidote for learned helplessness.

4
Feelings

Previously in this book, we have talked about locus of control, and how control plays such an important role in living a healthy life. You will remember when it comes to internal locus of control, or the things in life that we can control, there were three things-our thoughts, our feelings, and our behavior. I want to go into a bit more depth on the purpose of feelings and the role they play in healthy living.

As we have discussed, feelings are actually trailers to our thoughts. So how we think about something will determine what feeling shows up. But the relationship between thoughts and feelings is actually a two-way street. When you identify a feeling that you are having, you can actually trace it back to the thought from where it originated, and from there you can decide if that is a healthy way to think or not. Let's take a look and see how this might be a very useful tool for managing our thoughts and our feelings.

Imagine that you are driving to work and you find that you are gripping the wheel particularly tight and your jaw is clenched so tightly that you could bite a 10 penny nail in half. A quick check of the rest of your body finds that it is equally as tense. You reflect back on your morning, realizing that you were short with your spouse and you snapped at your child when she tried to show you her homework from the day before. Well, here is a newsflash for you . . . you are angry! I know that it sounds strange that a person would have all of the *symptoms* of anger without being able to connect the dots, but you would be surprised how often that is the case for many people. Men, in particular, are prone to having this experience since men are much more geared towards functional issues/concerns as opposed to experiential concerns like feelings.

OK, so you are angry. What do you do about it? Well, one thing you should do, if you don't know already, is to figure out the source of your anger. What is it that is making you angry? You run through what has been going on with you as of late, and there it is . . . your boss. Usually, he is really laid back and allows you a lot of autonomy to do your job, but for the last couple of weeks he has really been up your shorts! You have progressed from being slightly irritated to frustrated, and are now at full-blown anger. Great, so you are angry at your boss. So now what do you do? I would suggest that you trace that feeling right back to the thought from which it came. So you give it some thought, and the part that is really making you mad is that you feel he is questioning your ability to do your job, and that is not fair of him to do. After all, you have been a reliable employee for a lot of years at this place. So where does he get off questioning your competence now? A moment later you revisit your line of thinking. Is he really questioning my abilities (personalizing)? Then you consider the fact that business has been slow lately and he has been getting a lot of heat from his boss to get this project done. On top of that, his mother passed away a couple of months ago and his youngest daughter is getting ready to leave for college. Now that you are putting things in context you realize that he is not really questioning you, he is just under a lot of pressure himself, and he seems to be struggling. After giving this a bit more consideration you realize that you are no longer feeling angry. In fact, you are feeling sympathy for your boss and what it must be like to be in his shoes. You decide to go in and have a conversation with him to see if there is anything that you can do to help him out.

Well, that makes sense, but what if the situation was different? What if you realize you are angry with your boss, but your story reads like this . . . . You have been a good employee and your boss has been micromanaging you. Everything at the office has been the same except for the new guy they hired. He is a real know-it-all. He has not really done much since he got there, but tell everyone how smart he is, and he complains about things a lot. Your boss, for whatever reason, has been listening to this guy, and is now questioning everyone and what they do. The end result is he is way too involved in how you do your job. You run this one through the litmus test. You are doing the same quality work that you always have. Your boss is listening to this new guy, and in kind, is making your job a lot harder. That isn't really fair of him, so you realize that your anger is warranted. You decide to talk to your boss in an attempt to get him to "back off". If that doesn't work, you decide to polish up the old resume.

What I am trying to impart to you in this section is the importance of checking our thoughts as they relate to the feelings that we are experiencing. Quite often when we do this, the result is that you find your feelings are valid, and are based on a reasonable line of thinking. In these situations we can decide on a course of action to address the situation, or it may just be something that we need to let go. There are times, however, that checking out the thoughts associated to our feelings will result in us identifying thoughts that are not really very reasonable. Psychologists will often refer to these as *cognitive distortions*. When this is the case, you have to align your thinking with something more rational, and this will help to correct many errant emotions. Remember, feelings are trailers to thought. They do not go back and correct faulty thinking. If your thinking is flawed, chances are your emotions will be as well.

The best way to approach improving this area of your life is to become more *mindful* of your emotions. Mindfulness is kind of a buzzword in psychology today. Basically it means to become more aware of something on an ongoing basis. When I discuss emotions with my clients I will often draw the following analogy. Imagine that your feelings are the dashboard of your life. The emotions that you feel are like the gauges on your dash, each one serves a different purpose, and each one provides very important information regarding how you are doing in relation to the outside world. Quite often you look down at the gauges on the dashboard and everything is fine. Sometimes, however, we check the gauges and they indicate that we have to take action. The gas gauge gets close to "E" and it is time to pull in and fuel-up. Occasionally, the temperature gauge gets close to "hot" or the "Service Engine Soon" light comes on. In those situations more extensive repairs may be required.

To carry this analogy even further, think about how you check your gauges when you are driving. Hopefully you just glance down occasionally to see where things are at. Or if something lights up, that may capture a bit more of your attention, but your primary focus should be on the road ahead. It's the same way with being mindful of your emotions. You should not put living your life on hold so that you can spend the whole day getting in touch with your feelings. Life is not designed to go like that. When I discuss this with men, in particular, they will often begin to squirm in their seats. Many men would rather remove their own appendix with a butter knife than to spend time becoming more aware of their emotions. When this occurs, I ask the guy a question, "What would happen if you covered the gauges on your dashboard with a piece of cardboard and drove like that for a period of time?" The answer that they ultimately come to is that they would be okay for a while, but eventually they would suffer a breakdown on the side of the road. The same scenario applies for living your life being blind to your emotions. You will usually be alright for a while, but eventually it catches up to you. Some people who come to see me for counseling actually suffer a "breakdown", an emotional breakdown. Let me tell you one thing for sure. The people who have hit that critical period in their life are <u>very</u> receptive to the idea of the importance of emotions.

So let's say that you are driving along, living your life. You glance down and see that your "Service Engine Soon" light comes on. What should you do? Well, having worked my whole life in social service, I frequently find myself driving cars where one or more of the lights come on with regularity. Quite often there are more lights shining on my car's dashboard than the White House Christmas tree. When that happens with one of my cars, I usually call my best friend from childhood, Jeff Gardner. Now Jeff is a veritable virtuoso of the auto mechanic's world, and the first thing he asks me is my cap screwed on tight? Well, that seems like a rather personal question, but what he means in this situation is did I screw my *gas* cap on tight enough? A loosely secured gas cap can result in a "Service Engine Soon" light. An engine light can also be caused by a wire that has come loose, corrosion on an electrical connection, or a vacuum hose that has slipped off. When these things happen, there is not really anything significant going on with the car, the gauge is just receiving faulty information. This happens to us when we jump to conclusions, act impulsively, personalize things, or take things out of context. An emotion gets registered that should not really be there. In situations like this we need to correct the gauge (address our thoughts) rather than tear the engine apart (take action on the environment).

So what happens if the light comes on, you check it out, and it is not the result of a loose cap? Well, then it may be time for action. Depending on the emotion, and the situation at hand, you may need to take some corrective action to make a change in the situation. Sometimes that action is as simple as having a conversation with someone to tell them how you feel, or what you think. Other instances may require larger scale changes such as ending a relationship, changing jobs, or a behavior and/or lifestyle change.

Let's take a look at some emotions, and the important information that they are providing us. The emotions to follow are in no way an exhaustive list, but they are some of the more common emotions that people experience.

Anger-By far, anger is one of the most challenging emotions that people encounter. It is also one of the most misunderstood emotions that we have. People can respond to anger by becoming explosive and taking out their wrath on those around them, or they can hold their anger in and create a depression in which they implode on themselves. The natural purpose of anger is to protect us. It is the emotion that arises when we are in a situation where we are hurt by something or we are being treated unfairly. It provides us with ample energy to either stop what is hurting us, or to correct whatever is not fair. If you are standing in line at the movies and someone cuts in front of you it will make you angry because that is not fair. The anger provides you the energy to tap the person on the shoulder and direct them to the end of the line. Or, if a person is being mean or hurtful to you, it is anger that provides the energy to stand up for yourself and to tell them to stop. Without anger, you could go ahead and have "Welcome" printed on your forehead because everyone would treat you like a doormat.

Why does anger have such a bad reputation? The obvious answer is the potency of anger. Because anger is such a powerful emotion, many people will have the tendency to either shy away from its use or to overuse it. Even the Bible deals with the emotion of anger when God tells us "to be slow to anger". Now the careful observer will realize that the bible does not tell us to "not" get angry, just to be very judicious when we employ it. The effects of misusing anger can result in scarred childhoods, damaged relationships, lost employment, compromised health, and even death.

A term often misused when it comes to describing problems that people have with anger is when it is referred to as an "anger-control" problem. Unless the individual has suffered damage to their frontal lobe (the part of the brain responsible for curbing impulsive behavior) they do not have problem controlling their anger. Actually the opposite is true. People who are said to have an anger control problem are very good at using anger to control other people.

Think of one of these people in your life. We all have them. They are the person at school, or work, or even in your own home who goes ballistic at the slightest provocation. What do you and others think about them? Well, you probably think twice before you tell them something they will not like, or ask them something they will not want to do. That is the payoff for having an "anger control" problem. Now it does not come without a price tag. What you gain in being able to avoid what others might ask of you, you lose in the ability to maintain healthy relationships with them.

At times anger intensifies to the point of being uncontrollable, and irrational in nature. The volatility of this emotion is hard to manage, and is often referred to as rage. A factor that comes into play when this occurs is a part of our brain called the *sympathetic nervous system*. This is a very primitive part of our brain, and when used properly, is a great tool for protecting our well-being. The role of the sympathetic nervous system is to constantly monitor our environment for physical threats, like a dog running at us in an aggressive manner. When this situation is experienced the sympathetic nervous system is activated and a host of physiological responses occur. We get a shot of adrenaline, our heart rate increases, our blood pressure rises, breathing increases, blood gets directed into our large muscle groups, and we perspire. This is known as our *fight or flight response*. All the things that occur during this response help to prepare us to *fight* what is threatening us, or to take *flight* and get the heck out of there. If we go into *fight* mode we will experience anger or rage. This will provide the fuel to energize our response. If we go into *flight* mode we experience anxiety (we will discuss this momentarily). Either way we are preparing to handle a perceived attack.

I want to follow up this discussion of the sympathetic nervous system with a couple of thoughts. First, as I mentioned, the sympathetic nervous system is very primitive in nature. Because of this, it does not discriminate between a physical threat (like a dog charging us) and an emotional threat (like an argument with our spouse). All the features of the fight or flight response are much needed with a physical threat, but they are contraindicated when it comes to handling an emotional threat. Another feature that goes along with the sympathetic nervous response is a change in thinking. When our sympathetic nervous system is activated we can only focus on one thing, as our ability to consider a variety of options is compromised. Again, this works well with a physical threat, since you do not want to be considering the merits of five different options of behavior while a dog is galloping towards you. You want to think about one thing and put it into action. If you are in a conflict with your spouse, and you can only think of one thing, I can guarantee you that that one thing is not, "Boy, they are making some really good points!" Rather, the thoughts going through your mind will be, "Why don't you shut up?," "You are so unfair," "Why won't you leave me alone?".

As far as how to handle these kinds of situations in a healthy way, your best bet is to give yourself a "time-out". Remove yourself from the situation, go to someplace quiet or relaxing, and avoid thinking about the things that are angering you (or making you anxious). Health professionals tell us that it takes 25-30 minutes of being removed from the triggering event before we fully return to a calm state after the sympathetic nervous system is activated. As for wanting to resolve a conflict before you quiet the sympathetic nervous system, good luck with that. Neither *fight* nor *flight* is geared towards working cooperatively.

Anxiety-Anxiety is an emotion that can literally be disabling to people. Psychiatric conditions that primarily feature anxiety as their main symptom include Generalized Anxiety Disorder, Social Anxiety Disorder, various Phobias, and Post-Traumatic Stress Disorder just to name a few. The underlying issue with these, and other related disorders, is control. More specifically, people have a feeling of being out of control.

More often than not, when it comes to problems with anxiety, we are the creators and maintainers of our own problems. By this I mean that we send messages to ourselves that indicate that we need to control something that is actually out of our control.

This is often how people describe the experience of anxiety, it's a feeling of being "out of control". When we discussed control previously in regards to the locus of control, we said that there are really only three things in the world that we can control, our thoughts, feelings, and behavior. When we send the message to ourselves (consciously or unconsciously) that we must control something outside of those three things we create anxiety. We get anxious about what the weather will be like, we have angst over how much this or that will cost, we are anxious if that person doesn't seem to like us, or if that person is angry with us. We get anxious about when a plane will land, what traffic will be like, and what time dinner will be ready. In situations such as these, we pay a huge cost in emotional energy, and get nothing back but a sour stomach and a headache. In many ways it's like the old saying about worry. Worry is kind of like a rocking chair, it gives you something to do, but it doesn't really get you anywhere.

This is not to say that anxiety does not have a place, because there are times when it is called for (but even in these times, it does not really help us to handle situations better). Examples of situations where anxiety can be understood might include situations such as these: you are waiting on tests to determine the diagnosis of a medical condition, or if you have a sick child who is receiving medical attention, or if the mortgage is due and the funds are not there to pay it. Some people make a habit of being anxious about things that they have no need to do so. It's almost as if they tell themselves, unconsciously, that their worry or angst will somehow protect them from what it is that they are afraid.

For people who insist on being anxious over things that they cannot control, I will often suggest something for them to worry about. Sometimes I will challenge the chronic worrier with this scenario. How do they know that they are worrying enough? Maybe they are just at the tip of the iceberg with their worry, and they should be worrying much more than they actually are. Maybe if they worried more than they currently are they would reach the nirvana of worrying and they actually would be protected from anything bad happening. Maybe they are just getting started with their worrying. This, of course, brings to light the absurdity of worrying about things outside of our control.

For other lucky clients, I present them with a whole new thing to worry about, *blue ice.* Blue ice occurs when jet planes have leaky toilets. When they are soaring thousands of feet up in the air, under very cold temperatures, the liquid begins to freeze on the underside of the plane. Eventually, the block of blue ice reaches a large enough size to break free from the plane, and begins its decent to earth. As it falls, the block of frozen toilet water picks up speed until it reaches a terminal velocity. Eventually this large chunk of frozen waste will encounter some poor object on the earth's surface, and maybe that will be you. Imagine, you are sitting there worrying about whether you are accepted by this group of people or that group, or whether the car you drive is nice enough, then BLAMMO! You are crushed by blue ice! Kind of puts it all into perspective, doesn't it?

If people are dealing with anxiety, especially if it is clinically significant anxiety, and it is affecting your ability to function or to find peace in your life, I strongly encourage them to seek help. People can get some relief from focusing on locus of control issues, but clinically significant anxiety often requires professional intervention from a licensed counselor or psychiatrist. For many people being able to take a prescription anti-anxiety agent can allow them to relax to the point where they are receptive to therapy.

Depression-Depression is a very serious mental health condition, and every year it exacts a heavy toll on individuals, families, industry, and countries. The price tag for what is lost to depression comes in the form of dollars lost to decreased productivity of workers, diminished quality of life for individuals who suffer from depression and their families, and for many people who suffer from depression the price they pay is the ultimate one, death through suicide. In 2007 the number of lives lost in this country to suicide was 34,598 according to statistics compiled by the National Institute of Mental Health. That made it the tenth leading cause of death for that year (www.**nimh.nih. gov**/health/publications/**suicide-in**-the-us).

Depression, often referred to as the "common cold" of mental illness, is closely related to a feeling that we have previously discussed, anger. Clinically, depression is described as *repressed anger, stuffed anger, anger turned inward, or anger at the self.* When we discussed anger, it was described as a very potent emotion. A healthy outlet for anger is to be assertive, and to express your anger towards to person or situation that is making you angry. If that is not a possibility, then working through forgiveness and letting it go can be a healthy alternative. Stuffing it down and holding it inside can only turn out badly. When people determine that there is nothing that they can do about their situation, and they are not able to let it go, they often feel helpless and hopeless. These combine to create despair, which is a key ingredient in depression. Other symptoms of clinical depression include sleep disturbance (too little or too much), change in appetite (increase or decrease), lack of enjoyment of previously enjoyed activities, social isolation, irritability (particularly in the case of men and teens), frequent crying, increased difficulty managing self-care concerns, anxiety, feeling sad most of the time, decreased concentration, memory problems, and occasionally suicidal thoughts. People who are having suicidal thoughts or are actually contemplating suicide should seek immediate help from a mental health professional or from a hospital emergency room.

As a mental health condition, depression is a very treatable concern. Antidepressant medications, while not offering immediate relief like many forms of pain relievers, can offer considerable relief from the crushing pressures of depression. Therapy can assist people to identify their anger (many people suffering from depression do not identify the anger that they are repressing, or do not allow themselves to be angry). Once anger is identified it can be dealt with in some of the healthy manners previously discussed. In his book entitled "Change Your Brain, Change Your Life", Dr. Daniel Amen provides solid, concrete evidence for how the brain functions when a person is dealing with depression. He also offers some very practical techniques for how to make lifestyle changes to ward off depressive symptoms.

Again, many people will needlessly suffer from this debilitating condition out of not knowing about treatment options, or being fearful of the stigma associated with seeking help.

Fear-Fear is an emotion that, much like anger, is often misunderstood. If anger is poorly accepted due to its potency and potential for misuse, fear is misunderstood because of its correlation with weakness. When used properly, fear helps to protect us. When we perceive a threat in our environment the resulting emotion is fear. Fear creates a heightened sense of awareness, and may actually trigger our fight or flight mechanism. This response prepares us to best handle the threat to our person should we need to act. If we did not have fear we would place ourselves in harm's way, doing so with a complete lack of preparedness to handle a threat.

Two common problems that people have with the emotion of fear are misinterpreting something as a threat that is not threatening, and allowing fear to immobilize them.

Some people have a hair trigger when it comes to being fearful. They create fears for themselves that are not real or they magnify a threat so that it seems to be much bigger than it actually is. Imagine that someone had a very bad sore throat that just won't go away. They should go to the doctor for a prescription of an antibiotic to help their body fight off the infection. However, their grandfather died of throat cancer and his first symptom was a sore throat (of course he also smoked two packs of Lucky Strikes everyday as well). Fearing the diagnosis, the person avoids going to the doctor and suffers needlessly. I will often tell clients with this problem about the *boogeyman effect*. Young children who are having trouble sleeping by themselves will often create fears to corral their parents into tending to them or even allowing them to sleep with them if they can work it out. They will use the age-old story of the boogeyman in the closet. The very best thing a parent can do in this situation is to go to the closet with the child and turn on the light. No boogeyman can hold up to a closet light shone brightly. We need to do the very same thing with our irrational fears, shine some light on them. See if they hold up to scrutiny. If you can dispute a fear, pointing out its illogical nature you can gain power over it, and be free of it.

Secondly, people can allow fear to overwhelm them, making them, for all intents and purposes, totally ineffective. This condition is often referred to as *the deer in the headlights*. This is a very appropriate analogy for this situation. When you think about it, when a deer is crossing the road and sees a car's headlights, he has three choices. Two of the three choices actually turn out pretty well for the deer. First of all, the deer can just continue on across the road and can go on his merry way. Secondly, the deer can turn around and head back from where he came. Now this may mean he misses out on a cool drink of water or some tasty acorns, but he is still in one piece. It's the third choice that is the real problem for the deer, staying in the road. This will almost certainly end up badly for the deer (in addition for setting the stage for and *OnStar* commercial). When we allow fear to take control and immobilize us we are selecting option three and much like the deer, it usually means things are going to go bad.

The healthy use of fear first requires us to be attentive to our emotions. Using the dashboard analogy, we need to check our gages from time to time. When we sense fear we shouldn't be so quick to dismiss it as a sign of weakness. We also should not let it immobilize us. Rather, we should check out the thought from which it originated. If it holds merit, then we should prepare ourselves to handle the threat. If it doesn't, we should dismiss it, and get on with our lives. If you are a person who tends to have a faulty fear gage, you may want to try asking yourself a question. Ask yourself, "Is this something that I would recommend that someone I care dearly for be fearful of?" Typically, your first impulse to respond to this question is the right one. If you still aren't sure, ask someone that you trust what they think about your fear. Typically, with some practice in using these suggestions, you will get to be more effective in perceiving and managing your fear.

Happy-Wow, even though this is a book primarily dealing with troublesome emotions, there are actually some positive ones as well. Like many feelings, happy is frequently misunderstood as an emotion. I will ask clients early on in therapy what they want to get out of therapy, and they will typically respond with, "I just want to be happy." It's at this time I clarify for them that "happy" is not a very good goal to set for therapy. The reason is that happy is not a sustainable emotion. Happy is a transient emotion, and it is not designed to stick around indefinitely. Let's take a closer look at happy to see if we can gain a greater understanding of this emotion.

A few years back some researchers undertook a study to try to find the happiest country on earth. When the research concluded the findings were very surprising. The researchers determined that Denmark was actually the happiest country on earth. The surprise came from the fact that Denmark does not have the best weather around the globe, the food is not considered the tastiest, and it also does not boast the highest standard of living. The researchers found that what makes the Danish so happy is that they experience contentment with their lives. They are accepting and appreciative of what they have in life, and this frees them up to be happy. You see happiness is the emotion that we experience when the life that we are living features our priorities and our values. When the things that are most important to us are the centerpiece of our lives, it allows us to experience happiness.

Since no life can have this set of circumstances on a continuing basis, happiness is a very transient emotion. Many people experience a chronic lack of happiness in their lives. Even people with ample money and worldly goods can experience chronic unhappiness. If this describes you, or if you have a hard time remembering the last time that you were happy, it is time to take a hard look at your life. Maybe you have been spending too much time chasing after the things that the world says is important, and not enough time with the things that are important to you. Think back to the last time that you remember being happy, or spend time sorting through what is really most important to you. Find a way of constructing a life that features more acceptance and contentment. This does not mean that you should become complacent or unmotivated, just never forget that which you cherish the most.

Hurt-Hurt is an emotion that we experience when someone says or does something mean or inconsiderate and it is directed towards us. Hurtful behaviors might be calling us a name, sharing confidential information, or just plain showing disregard for how something might affect us. Hurt can often come from disappointment, or when we have expectations of someone or something that are not met.

Hurt is one of the most common reasons that people have relationship problems. When you enter into a committed relationship, such as a marriage for example, people have certain expectations. These expectations might include being held at a certain status in the other person's life (being honored), being protected by the other, and having the needs that you have in the relationship be met in a reasonable fashion. When these things do not occur, the person is disappointed. This will often set off a domino effect that can be damaging and even deadly to relationships. Disappointment results in hurt, hurt gives way to anger, anger devolves into resentment, and resentment becomes the mortar that builds the walls dividing people.

In healthy relationships, the individuals can take situations where they are hurt and use them to improve their relationship. By communicating how you feel to your partner, and what your experience of the situation was that resulted in you getting hurt, you can develop the skills to avoid those situations in the future. I am not suggesting that relationships will ever be able to get to the point where no one's feelings will ever be hurt in a relationship. The fact is that from the moment you bring two people together in a relationship the clock is ticking until someone gets hurt. The key is the magnitude of the hurt. There is a difference between bumped or bruised feelings, and a devastating emotional injury.

Lonely-Lonely is a feeling that can be particularly painful. Loneliness is often used interchangeably with a related emotion, feeling alone. The truth is, lonely and alone are different emotions. Feeling alone means that you are by yourself, and no one else is around. Feeling lonely means that you desire a connection with another person (or people) and you do not have one. Therefore, you certainly can feel lonely when you are alone, but you can also feel lonely when you are in a room full of people. In fact, it is more painful to feel lonely when you are around others, or in a marriage, than when you are literally alone and by yourself. The added pain comes from the fact that you desire a connection with another person who is present, but you just don't have that connection.

If a person is feeling lonely, just like any other emotion, it is telling them something . . . to get connected with others. If you do not have other people in your life, seek them out. Join a church, a synagogue, or some other house of worship. Explore what is happening in your local park district or YMCA. Get involved with a volunteering experience, or join a local political movement. Feeling lonely does not have to be a terminal condition, but it usually involves stepping out of your comfort zone in order to let others into your life.

If you are in a relationship/marriage and you are lonely, that is telling you something as well. Again, you have to take action, as these circumstances do not correct themselves. Challenge yourself and your partner to reinvest in the relationship, and do so with a sense of urgency. If your partner is not of the mind to do so at this moment, don't allow that to detour you. Relationships are systems, and like any system, when you change one part of it the other will change to accommodate it (as long as the original change remains constant). Time is a precious commodity, and you don't want to spend one more minute than you have to experiencing loneliness.

Rejection-Rejection is a very painful emotion. In fact the fear of rejection is often what is behind the lonely person's avoidance of trying to engage with others. Understanding humans for the social beings that they are, I believe that the fear of rejection is often experienced by people as a terror rather than a garden-variety fear. Humans require other humans to survive. We are not like sea turtles that hatch and then make their way to the ocean. Even the social recluse who lives in a shack out in the Montana wilderness relied on other humans to reach adulthood. Modern society offers us the opportunity for survival without routine interaction with others, but that has not always been the case. In earlier times in our history to be excluded from the group meant a sentence of death. I believe that this was (and is) such a powerful force in our lives that it has actually imprinted itself on us on a cellular level. We see this fear grip us throughout the life cycle from the young child who is not included in a game, to a teen rejected by a love interest, to the pain of being abandoned in a relationship, to the elderly person's fear of being placed in a home and forgotten. Yes, rejection is a very powerful emotion.

If you have experienced rejection, or have avoided relationships for fear of being rejected, do not allow this to control you. When we allow this to happen we are often engaging in "learned helplessness" as previously described in the work of Martin Seligman. If you are insecure or lack confidence in your abilities to develop relationships, challenge yourself. If you feel that this is too big a task to encounter on your own, seek out a competent therapist to help you develop these skills. Do not allow yourself to become a prisoner to these emotions.

Sadness-Sadness is yet another emotion that many people are challenged to deal with in their lives. The purpose of sadness is to indicate that a person is dealing with a loss. That loss can be concrete in nature, such as the loss of a loved one, the loss of a job, or the loss of one's previous status through financial problems or foreclosure. The loss can also be more experiential in nature as well. A person can be sad if they do not feel as connected with their spouse, children, or friends. A person can also feel sad when they move through what psychologists call phase of life issues such as leaving home for the first time, graduating from school, having children grow up and leave home, or retiring from a job that you have worked for many years.

In some ways sadness is unique in that experiencing sadness does not mean that a person can motivate themselves to correct the situation that is making them feel sad. Surely, if you are not feeling as close as you used to be to a family member or a friend, you can put forth effort to reclaim that lost closeness. But all the sadness in the world will not bring back a loved one who has died, a home lost to fire, or a job that was "down-sized". This unique quality of sadness makes it a challenging emotion for people to try to manage. It is a reminder of something important that we have lost. Ideally, over time, the sadness is replaced by sweeter memories of what has been lost in the case of death, or a new job or a new home takes the painful sting out of what is no more.

Some people, when dealing with the powerlessness of sadness, will swear off letting anything new into their lives. They are done with relationships following a divorce. They will never have another pet because it hurts to much when they die. As a therapist, when I hear these things from clients, I will often challenge them with a hypothetical deal. I ask them, "What if I could make all the pain from your loss go away in an instant?" This usually peaks their attention. "However", I continue, "it means you will also have to give up all the special memories of time spent with that person (or pet). It also means that the children that you shared with your spouse will no longer exist. Or the accomplishments and relationships formed at the job you lost would never have happened. Would you take it?" Usually, with some reflection the person realizes that the good times and memories outweigh the sadness, and they realize that if they would have been closed off to new opportunities in the past they never would have had the good times they are missing now. That, and time, often frees people up to re-engage in life.

The feelings that were explored in this chapter are a mere handful of the total spectrum of emotions that people can experience. In my clinical experience these emotions tend to be some of the more common, and more challenging, emotions for people to deal with in their lives. It can be well worth the effort for a person (men in particular) to increase their vocabulary of feeling words. This can promote greater self-awareness and understanding, as well as improve your ability to relate to people with whom you have a close relationship.

One final thing about emotions is to remember the example used earlier that feelings are like the gauges on the dashboard of our life. Now think about how you drive your car. You do not drive with your eyes fixed to the gauges (unless you are on 'E' and are looking to make it to the next gas station). Your thoughts are telling you where to go, not your temperature gauge. Therefore, don't be led by your emotions. Remember, they can often be faulty. Rather, use your emotions as information with which to make decisions in your life.

5
Don't Be A Turkey

As you can probably tell by now, I am quite an animal lover, and as such, many of the stories that I tell to clients to get a lesson across to them will involve animals. Many years ago, I would regularly visit the state of South Dakota in the summer. One of the activities that I would enjoy during these trips was fishing, and there was always plenty to be had on these trips. On the way to the lake from the place where I would stay was a large turkey farm. Every day I would drive by this place and I was always struck by the sight of seemingly thousands of turkeys standing at the barn opening pressed up against this thin fence which separated the turkeys from freedom.

This scene bore a striking resemblance to a mass of teenagers waiting to get into a general admission rock concert. I mean these turkeys up front by the fence were bearing the full pressure of the entire "turkey nation" just pushing to get out of the barn and on their way to wherever turkeys desire to go. In my more twisted moments I would envision these turkeys playing out scenes from *Shawshank Redemption,* and one of them narrating with the voice of Morgan Freeman. But I digress . . . anyway, one day I drive by this farm and one of the turkeys has made it! He is standing free and clear on the outside of the fence (Andy Dufresne had made it!).

This story would have a wonderful ending if the turkey had high-tailed it down the road, following the turkey version of the underground railroad, struggling to gain his freedom and to start a new life for himself, but sadly it doesn't. You see, that turkey, who had finally made it to the other side of the fence did nothing but stand there at the fence pushing back on the fence from the outside. He had tried his whole life to get out, but once he got there he had no plan, so he did what he had always done, stand there with the other turkeys.

Change is something that many people desire for their lives, but few know how to effectively bring this about in a meaningful way. The truth is that many people are afraid of change, and will take strong measures to resist it, even healthy change. A second problem that people have with change is that they have the distorted belief that it is impossible to bring about change in their lives. And a third problem that people will have with change is lacking a plan that will allow them to successfully change.

When my daughter Amanda was young we lived in a house in Braidwood, IL with a lovely view of a small lake at the end of the property. I built a wooden swing set in the back yard for her to play on and I covered the ground under the swing set with shredded wood mulch to soften the falls that would inevitably occur. Amanda loved this swing set and would often run to the edge of the mulch, take off her shoes, and get to swinging. It would be a short while after this that Amanda would realize something. You see wood mulch and bare feet do not a good combination make. She had slivers in her feet.

Now any parent who has encountered a situation where their child has a foreign object slid into their skin will understand the trauma that ensues. The procedure for correcting this condition can be very trying on the parent-child relationship. One does not require a second opinion by Dr. Gregory House to understand that these objects have to come out, and this will involve a fair amount of pain to accomplish this. Both Amanda and I knew that these things had to be pulled out, but she was afraid of what had to occur to accomplish this.

So there I am, tweezers in one hand and a sweaty four-year-old's foot in the other. As I make my initial approach there is a screech followed by the foot being yanked from my hand. I offer some words of encouragement, reacquire the foot, and proceed with attempt number two. Bam, same thing happens. Well, this dance between Amanda and myself went on for the better part of eternity with me getting more frustrated, her getting more afraid, and that foot getting more slippery. At somewhere along this process I imparted some wisdom that I hoped would gain me a little more cooperation. I told Amanda, "OK, I guess we will just leave those splinters in there until they get infected. Then it will really hurt when we have to take them out." Now folks, I want you to appreciate that this moment is the culmination of seven plus years of college, graduate, and post-graduate schooling that has allowed me to concoct this grave story to manipulate this little kid. Chalk one up for the parents! Well, eventually the splinters came out and I am glad to say that Amanda is none the worse for the wear.

This story really captures the experience of many of the people who come to see me for counseling. They are in pain and something is present in their life that is causing that pain (just like the splinter in that little foot). They really want to change, but they are afraid. Now this seems to fly in the face of logic. As we have seen earlier in this book, pain and discomfort are usually prime motivators for change. If you were to sit on a chair that had a pin sticking in it, that would be a huge motivator for you to change your position and quickly. This is not always the case with emotional pain. Many people will continue to endure emotional pain for years, not because they grow comfortable with it, because let's face it, pain is pain. Rather, they grow familiar with it, and they are afraid to change.

Alfred Adler was famous for saying that people in need of counseling are people who are discouraged. Now think about that word for a moment. The word literally means dis-couraged, to disconnect from your courage. You see, when it comes to fear, the best antidote around is courage. Adler would also say that one of the primary roles of the counselor is to encourage their client, or to help them to reconnect with their courage. We are all born with all of the courage that we will ever need for our entire lives. Now you may be saying, "Oh yeah? How can you say that if you don't even know me or anything about me?" Well, that is true, but I do know that if you are reading this book, you have somehow made it this far in life. That means that you have never encountered anything in your life, not one single thing, which you have not been able to handle. Now like all of us, you may look back and say that you wished you would have handled some things better or at least differently, but somehow you handled them.

Another way to look at this idea of inborn courage can be seen in most of our lives at around one year of age. This is the time when most of us (barring a health complication) learn to walk. Think of this process through the eyes of the child. Imagine that you are standing there holding onto a person or a piece of furniture for support. Now you have to let go and take that first step. If you are like most children at this point you topple over on your face. The amazing thing is that those young children have such a drive to master walking that they keep doing it over and over again with many spills along the way. Take a moment to think about that as an adult. Imagine that you are in that same situation where you are taking a step or two and then crashing to the ground. How would that be for you? I am guessing pretty scary as well as being ripe with discouragement. That is more proof that the courage that we need to take on any challenge in life is born into us. Unfortunately, many of us disconnect with that courage throughout the course of our lives. With these examples in mind, the question is not whether you can handle what you are facing in your life, but how well you are going to handle it. All you have to do is access your courage to start the process.

We have spoken previously in this book about the power of thought, and how easy it is for people to handicap themselves by entertaining distorted or irrational thoughts. This point is so pivotal in the message that I am trying to get across I want to revisit it again. Of course we will return to the world of animals for a story to get us started.

Circus elephants are massive and powerful animals. Their strength is legendary, and some estimate that if an elephant could do the human equivalent of a bench press they would be able to lift over 4,000 pounds. Nonetheless, these colossal beasts can often be contained by using a wooden stake pounded in the ground and a relatively thin piece of rope. Considering the physics of this circumstance, the elephant should be able to yank up the stake or snap the rope and be well along the same underground railroad that the turkeys could follow, but the elephant does not go anywhere. The reason is that the elephant is being contained by his beliefs much more than the rope. When a baby elephant is born in captivity, and it will eventually need to be contained in this manner, it is trained through a process known as tethering. The elephant is fitted around its right front leg with a shackle that is attached to a heavy chain which is in turn attached to a large block of concrete. The elephant's initial response to this situation is to struggle and struggle to try to break free. Eventually, however, the elephant will stop its struggle and accept that it is pointless to try to get loose. Shortly after this occurs you can contain this animal with a piece of rope tied to the same leg that is affixed to a wooden stake. You see, the elephant holds the belief that struggling is pointless at this point, so why bother? Sadly, many of us are tethered by the same kinds of distorted and irrational beliefs.

These beliefs take many forms, but all of them are damaging. There is the child who does not try out for the baseball team because they know they will never get picked. Then we have the student who does not pursue a medical degree because they believe that they are not smart enough. Of course there is the actor/actress who does not try out for a part because "they would never choose anyone like me". And let's not forget the guy who doesn't ask out the woman he is interested in because "she would never go out with a guy like me". One that I have recently encountered goes like this, "why would I write a book since no one would probably read it?" Well, let's just say I am hoping that the last one isn't true.

Now let me make something clear. I am not one of those who say, "Dream it and you can make anything occur". Unfortunately, we all have this little thing called reality that comes into play. I may have played four years of high school football, but the likelihood that I was going to play in the NFL was zero. That is not because it is impossible to do so, but rather the combination of my skill set, my physical attributes, my level of desire to perfect my skills, and my want to pursue other goals in my life. In my own case, I believe that I could get into medical school or law school if I chose to dedicate myself to working towards that. I also could probably run for political office of some sort if I had a want to do so. I simply have chosen not to do so in my life. I never once told myself that I could not do these things. Are there things in your life that you are not pursuing because you have tethered yourself to a false belief? If that in any way describes you, challenge yourself. Honestly ask yourself "why not?" rather than just resigning yourself to a belief about something that is just not true.

A truly inspiring story that drives this point home is the story of Jim Abbott. Jim Abbot was a baseball pitcher. He pitched for the University of Michigan, pitched on the 1988 Olympic gold medal winning baseball team, pitched in the major leagues from 1989 to 1999, and even threw a no-hitter for the New York Yankees over the Cleveland Indians in 1993. All of this biographical data would be impressive for any person, to be sure. But there was something unique about Jim Abbott that made him different from most people who have played in the major leagues. Jim Abbott was born with one arm. When I think about what Jim Abbott was able to accomplish in his life with one arm, I often imagine that over the course of his baseball life there must have been whispers (many of which he heard) saying, "Sure he can play little league like that, but he won't be able to go much farther." Similar words were probably uttered when he was in high school and college. All it would have taken to derail this remarkable story would have been for Jim Abbott to listen to just one of these non-believers. That's it . . . . end of story . . . no gold medal . . . no no-hitter . . . nothing. Disputing illogical/irrational thoughts is a key step in removing a common road block to achieving success.

The final factor that people need to consider when it comes to change is their plan. Insurance agents around the country are famous for saying, "In life no one plans to fail, but many people fail to plan." Unfortunately, both of these approaches often lead to undesirable results.

6

Feel Like You Are In A Rut?

Humans, in large part, are creatures of habit. We often settle into patterns of behavior, and unless we experience some obvious negative consequences, it just becomes what we do. These patterns might be as benign as how we brush our teeth or put on a shirt, to the damaging effects of our nasty "habit" of "dealing" with stress by getting drunk/high, eating the top three rows of food in the fridge, or gambling away the mortgage. The list of destructive behaviors that people employ to avoid dealing with situations is endless. The one thing that they have in common is the ability to destroy the lives of those who engage in these behaviors, and those who love and care for them.

In the old west, a common form of transportation was the wagon train. In a wagon train, one wagon would follow along behind the next on the way to their destination. The wheels on these wagons were uniformly measured, and because they would follow along in these long lines, grooves would form in the earth. The wagon wheels would settle into these grooves over time so that wherever the grooves went, that is where the wagon would go. This works out well if you like the destination where they are leading, but if you wanted to head in a different direction you are out of luck.

Our brains operate in a very similar fashion. Neuro-pathways form in our brains from repeated patterns of behavior or thought. This allows for a network of neurons in the brain to connect in a way that facilitates learning. When a particular neuro-pathway is used repeatedly it will develop into a default position in our brain. Much like the grooves in the earth formed by the repeated traffic from the wagon wheels, once you start, you know where it will end. To demonstrate this point I want to ask you to clasp your hands together with your fingers intertwined with each other. Now, without looking, what thumb do you have on top? Whichever it is, it did not happen by accident. If I asked you to do it one hundred times, you would probably have the same thumb on top for all one hundred tries. Let's try something a little different. With your hands clasped together as before, switch your thumbs so that the other thumb is now on top. Feels kind of awkward, huh? That is because you stepped out of the familiar. And if you are like most people, you are probably feeling an urge to switch your thumbs back to the familiar way. Again, this is a very common occurrence.

If I were to suggest to you that I wanted you to force yourself to rehearse holding your hands clasped together with your opposite thumb on top, and you did so trial after trial, day after day, that would eventually become the new "typical" way that you hold your hands. But, you might ask, what happens to the grooves in the earth? What happens to the old behavior pattern that persisted so long in your life? Well, much like those grooves in the earth, they are still there. And if you move the *wagon* that is your life too close to those old ruts you will slip back in. Psychologists refer to this occurrence as "spontaneous recovery", that is when an old pattern of behavior that has been extinguished suddenly reappears. Or occasionally, the reappearance of an old behavior can be the result of state/situation dependent learning. This is when the ex-smoker experiences stress and starts yearning for a smoke, or someone who has quit drinking finds themselves faced with a "beer run" while at a baseball game. Each can be particularly challenging to the person who is trying to kick the habit. I do want to emphasize that I said *challenging*, and not *impossible*.

Behavioral scientists tell us that it takes about three weeks to create a habit, or to change a behavior. I would say that if a person really wants to be successful with eliminating an unhealthy behavior, that it takes even longer than that. I am not trying to be discouraging to those who desire change, just realistic. When clients come to see me with problem patterns of behavior I will quickly discuss with them the difference between a behavior change and a lifestyle change. A lifestyle change leaves the individual with a great chance for success, while with a behavior change the clock is ticking until the person is back in their rut.

What is the difference between a lifestyle change and a behavior change besides how long they last? It's actually pretty simple. Let's take for an example someone who is struggling with problem drinking and they are looking to correct the problem. The person who is attempting to do this with a behavior change will come up with a plan that simply says, "I am not going to drink again." And the truth is, the person really does mean it at the time they say it, but this is a short-term solution for a long-term problem. If this person had that much self-discipline they would probably not be a problem drinker to begin with. Now let's take a look at a person who addresses this concern with a lifestyle change.

The person making a lifestyle change puts the issue on project status. They start out to understand the purpose of the behavior, or in other words, what it does for the person. Say the person uses it to escape pressure. Then the person needs to develop the skills to deal with the pressures head-on. If the drinking helps the person to deal with anxiety or some other emotional problem in their life, they need to make some changes in life to reduce the anxiety or get into therapy to develop more tools to deal with life in a healthier way. Perhaps the person drinks when they get bored. Then they have to finds healthier sources of excitement. You get the drift, find the purpose the problem behavior is serving and create a healthy alternative to the addiction.

The next step in a lifestyle change is to create your plan of attack. The plan you come up with to address the problem should have both a reactive and a proactive component. The reactive part of the plan is the "in case of emergency, break glass" part of the plan. So when a situation comes up where you are tempted to engage in the unhealthy behavior, what are you going to do differently? This part of the plan has to be ready to be put into action at the first sign of temptation. Don't wait until you are in that position to try to throw something together. By that time you will be moving to your default position, and your wagon is back in the rut.

The proactive part of the plan is what you do even before the problem situation presents itself. Alcoholics Anonymous is famous for talking to alcoholics about "people, places, and things". In other words, you have to examine these areas of your life and make changes accordingly. If there are people that you have hung out with to drink, you have to let them go unless they are willing to be part of the solution, and not part of the problem. "Places" means that you have to steer clear of places associated with the problem behavior. Alcoholics should not go to liquor stores or bars. I know that seems obvious, but not so to a person who is struggling to end their romance with alcohol. "Things" relates to the concern of avoiding activities that involve drinking. Maybe that means weekend fishing trips, because you would always bring a twelve pack with you. Maybe helping your neighbor work on his car isn't such a good idea because this would lead to a late-night drink fest. I realize that I am talking about a lot of change, but again, if these problems were that simple, people would not have difficulties in dealing with them. Also, these changes don't all have to be depriving yourself of something. You can find other things to do that you enjoy, or adjust the things that you do to make sure that you exclude drinking. Remember the definition of insanity: "To continue to do the same thing and to expect a different result."

The last components of a lifestyle change are commitment and accountability. Most people these days are commitment averse.

Coming from the microwave generation myself, I understand that people often want quick results, and if they don't get them, they ditch the plan and move onto the next one. If you are serious about addressing problems of this magnitude, you have to sign on for the good times and the bad. It's not all going to be seashells and balloons. There will be times when things feel pretty crappy, and there will be a strong desire to quit and go back to what is familiar. Unless you are willing to see this thing through, even if it gets hard, be honest with yourself that you are not ready to change. Finally, make yourself accountable to someone besides yourself. This is an essential part of any successful plan because we all know just what to say to let ourselves off the hook. We make deals with ourselves, excuse things "just this one time", and so on. Think of someone who will not let you off the hook. If your mother would tell you that it's OK that you didn't follow through, she is not the one. If your friend is struggling with the same, or similar, problem, he's probably not the one. A spouse who has enabled you throughout this whole process is probably not a good choice either. It has to be someone who will hold your feet to the fire. Because of this, getting involved in a twelve step program and/or working with a qualified therapist can be incredibly helpful. These individuals are knowledgeable about the problem with which you are dealing, and can maintain objectivity in their dealings with you.

I don't often work with individuals who participate in addictive behaviors, but from time to time I do, and here is what I tell them. First of all, they do not *suffer* from an addiction, they participate in one. I know that right now addiction counselors who might be reading this are ready to ring my neck, but hear me out. Addictive behaviors do involve choice. I understand that, especially with substance abuse, there are physical components to these conditions. If a person is physically dependent on a drug, they do require medical attention to get through the acute phase of their recovery. Once they are out of this phase, it is a matter of choice. The alcoholic chooses to pull into the liquor store, the crack addict chooses to drive to that side of town, and the smoker chooses to buy the pack at the gas station. People really need to get over this idea of being a victim. Believe me, being labeled a victim is vastly overrated.

When I work with people on their addictions, they will often feel sorry for themselves or get angry with the fact that they can't go here or they can't do that because of their addiction. At this time I always pose to them the following suggestion: "I want you to go to a ward in a hospital where they are caring for people with terminal cancer. Then I want you to offer to switch conditions with them. Tell them that you will assume their terminal condition where there is no hope for getting well, and they can have your addiction. All they have to do is take action to deal with their addiction, and they can live a healthy life." Now tell me how many people on that ward would switch places in a heartbeat. Success rates for people with addictions are abysmal, and this is because more people are enthralled with the idea of being sober than are willing to commit to it. Maybe that sounds a bit harsh, but you have a hard time arguing with the logic.

Throughout much of this section I have referenced problem drinking, but to be honest, you can cut and paste any type of addictive behavior where alcohol is mentioned. Maybe your drug of choice is some illegal street drug or prescription medications. Maybe you gamble excessively, smoke cigarettes, shop excessively, have an addiction to pornography, or maybe working too much is a place where you escape. Whatever it might be, it is incumbent on you, for your sake, and those who care for you to get this thing fixed. If you really want to pull your life out of the rut that you are in, and head in a different direction it takes real hard work. You will make mistakes and occasionally come up short, but you have to maintain your commitment. There are no easy solutions to these problems. If easy solutions did actually exist, then everyone would be using it, and I would be selling appliances somewhere. Be honest with yourself, be ready to commit, and develop a solid plan to change your lifestyle with the help of individuals who are qualified to help.

7

Spring Cleaning For The Soul

One of the issues that people who see me for counseling struggle with most frequently is dealing with the crushing weight of past hurts, resentments, and residual anger. Over a lifetime, an individual could potentially accumulate enough emotionally toxic material to rob them of the ability to live a healthy and free life. Over my more than twenty years meeting with individuals, couples, and families who are at the darkest moments of their lives, I have heard first-hand accounts of actual horror stories. From gut-wrenching accounts of children being abused physically, emotionally, and sexually, to tales of betrayal and infidelity in marriage, from parents who buried their children due to drunk-driving accidents to loved ones dealing with the dramatic effects of a loved one's traumatic brain injury, I have had a front row seat to many of life's atrocities. And while I am always inspired by the shear emotional strength that these individuals display just getting through the day with these experiences weighing on them, I am also struck by how much they struggle with the concept that I present to them that can help to ease the burden. The key to healing from these, and any other painful experience in life, is forgiveness.

I have to admit, that I actually have to tap into my own courage in working with individuals when I broach the subject of forgiveness with people who have suffered at the hands of another, or through some catastrophic twist of fate. The pain and anguish in their eyes sends a clear message . . . "Do Not Enter". But if I am going to ask them to face these emotional demons, I must also demonstrate a willingness to venture with them on this journey. Once their initial protest that "there is no way I can forgive what has happened" is made, I try to clarify for them what forgiveness is, and what it is not. People will often confuse forgiveness with the related concepts of *excusing* and *forgetting.*

More than anything, people get stuck on the concept of forgiveness when they equate it with excusing, and it's easy to see why. If you have been hurt or injured by the actions of another the mere thought of excusing it minimizes what you have experienced in either physical or emotional pain. Some examples of excusing might be as follows: "My mom used to beat us with the belt because that is the way that she was raised", "Uncle Rich sexually abused me because he was molested as a child", "Dad never supported my plans for my life because grandpa never supported him", "The guy who drove drunk and killed my aunt was hurting because his wife is dying of cancer", or "The kids at school bully me because they have low self-esteem themselves." No, no, no . . . .a thousand times no! While these, and many others, might be explanations, they are in no way excuses. If a person had a bad childhood themselves due to abuse or neglect, then it is up to them, when they become an adult, to take responsibility for their lives and get the help they need to stop the damage these experiences inflicted. If a person is struggling with stress at home or on the job, they need to find healthy ways to deal with these concerns so that they do not take them out on others. All too often in my line of work I encounter generational patterns of abuse, neglect, or general maltreatment. Well, I am here to tell you that it is each individual's responsibility to assume control of their own lives, and to make corrections, as needed, to live their lives in the healthiest way possible.

Quite often, after discussing this perspective with clients, they will still protest that if all the person has been exposed to as a child is unhealthy behavior, then how are they supposed to just "get their lives right"? Let's look at it like this. When a child is growing up, they are like little sponges absorbing everything that they can from their environment, both good and bad. If you think about the role that parents play in this process it's almost like they are architects who are helping the child to construct a blueprint for how to live their lives. Unfortunately for some children, since they cannot competitively "bid out the job", the parents they have are the only ones with whom they can work. Therefore, distorted, unhealthy, toxic, and often dangerous patterns of thought go into the blueprint. When the child becomes an adult, they take ownership of these prints, and it becomes their guidelines for how to construct their lives. Now let's follow this example one step further. The individual who has just taken ownership of the prints begins to apply them in their approach to life as an adult. They roll out the drawings and in looking them over they realize a couple of things. The house, as it is drawn, has an incomplete foundation, it is facing the wrong direction in relation to the street, and there is no front door (if this were an actual architect it's time to cancel the check!). The person can now do one of two things. They can go ahead and build the house according to the drawings, or they can modify the drawings so that it will be the way that it is supposed to be. It is for this reason that even if a person had an unhealthy upbringing it is not an excuse to be used to hurt or mistreat others.

Forgiveness is not forgetting. When someone wrongs you, or they are hurtful or abusive to you, those are real events that are a matter of history. They cannot and should not be forgotten. Your life is not like a dry erase board that someone can come along and deface with defamatory remarks and then have it simply wiped clean. Many hurts and abuses, especially of the magnitude with which we are discussing, leave an indelible mark on the person's mind and soul. As a matter of fact, forgetting them (if you could) might put you at risk for repeated injury at the hands of toxic people. Let's take a look at a scenario that illustrates this. Imagine that I am an acquaintance of yours, you know me, just not very well. I approach you with a wonderful investment opportunity that will double your money in a week's time, and all I need from you is an initial "investment" of $5,000. You hear my pitch, and you would sure like an extra 5K in the bank so you write me the check. Well, quick as a wink, I am off to the bank to cash it, and then it's off to Las Vegas. I play poker, roulette, blackjack, and the slots, and within 4 hours your "investment" is toast. I see you at the end of the week and you are eagerly awaiting your return on the "investment". I decide to just be straight with you, and to tell you the error of my ways. Even though I did not think I would lose your money, and I really did believe that I could double it and then some, I have nothing for you. You are angry, and you have every right to be. Now here is where the forgive/forget part comes in. It would be healthy for you to forgive me for what happened (maybe not immediately, but eventually) because if you don't, it is you who will carry the burden of my misbehavior. I will probably be off swindling someone else and you are stuck with the hurt, anger, and resentment related to my actions. And here is why it is not wise to *forget* actions such as these. Let's say a year goes by and I approach you again with another "fool-proof investment"... There you have it.

Before we move on to the process of forgiveness, I want to address a matter regarding the Christian view of forgiveness. The bible, which possesses wisdom far beyond what you will find in the pages of this book, calls on all of us to be forgiving of each other. As a matter of fact, our own forgiveness is dependent on our ability to forgive others (Forgive, and ye shall be forgiven Luke 6:37). The bible also tells us that if we accept Christ as our savior, that on the day of judgment our sins will be forgotten. Believe me when I say that I understand this, and I do not feel that I am being hypocritical. Ideally, we could forget the harm that another has brought on us, but on earth, that leaves us vulnerable.

Therefore, we will work through forgiveness now, and save the forgetting for a time when we are in a far better place.

Once a person is able to move beyond whether they are willing or able to forgive, they often state that they do not know *how* to work through the process of forgiveness. Really the question that is more challenging than *how* to forgive is *am I ready to forgive?* Forgiveness, in simple terms, is just letting go of the hurt, anger, and resentment associated with an emotional wound. Determining if you are emotionally in a place where you can let go of the pain is another question entirely. You see emotional pain, just like physical pain, serves a purpose. Let me provide an example that will illustrate this point. Imagine that you were walking down the sidewalk and you accidentally stepped in a hole in the sidewalk and your ankle twists. You hear a "pop" from your ankle followed by searing pain. That pain, as bad as it feels, actually serves a very healthy function. As long as your ankle is that painful, you are not going to be walking on it any further until you get some treatment for it. Imagine that you did not have that pain to warn you of the damage and the risk of further injury that walking on a broken ankle would do. That would not be a pretty picture. Therefore, the pain serves the healthy purpose of protecting you from further injury. Now let's take this example one step further (pun intended). Let's say that rather than getting proper treatment for your ankle, you decide to just numb it up with Novocain. That way you can keep on walking without the pain, but the root problem of the broken bone is steadily getting worse. This is exactly what people do who turn to alcohol, drugs, or any of a host of other addictive behaviors to avoid dealing with issues.

So when you suffer an emotional wound, the pain that results actually serves the purpose of not putting yourself into a position of being reinjured. It keeps the person who injured you at bay so that you don't let them back into your heart to do more damage. Returning to our parallel example of the broken ankle, as long as there is a risk for further injury, the emotional pain still serves a purpose. Once, however, the risk of further emotional damage is reduced by eliminating that person from your life, or at least having healthier boundaries with them, then you are in a position to forgive.

The Cost of the Cast

At the risk of over-using this comparison between physical hurts and emotional hurts, I want to proceed with the example of the broken ankle because it really brings to light what goes into forgiveness. So you are in the ER and the pain is really hard to take. You are being wheeled around because any further pressure on that damaged joint will only make the matter worse. When the doctor finally sees you he confirms there is a break and your ankle is set and put into a cast. Let's take a look at the role the cast plays in the healing process. The cast will afford you an added layer of protection for the damaged joint to protect it from further injury, but it does so at a cost. If you ever have had to sport a cast yourself, you know what I am talking about. What you gain in increased safety, you give up in function. Getting dressed is now a trick. Bathing is a challenge. Driving may be out of the question for a while. No softball or jogging will be on your schedule for a while. Those are all the functions that you cannot perform while you require the security of the cast.

Once the bone fuses back together and the risk of re-injury is reduced, the cast itself actually becomes harmful to the person wearing it. Due to the lack of functional use of the limb, the muscles inside the cast have gradually been atrophying, literally withering away. It is at this point that the cast must be removed to avoid permanent loss of functioning. As you might have guessed, removing the cast is the process of forgiving. People who have been hurt emotionally erect walls around their heart that serve that same self-protecting function that the cast does for the broken ankle. The walls around the heart are made up of hurt, anger, and resentment rather than plaster of paris. When a person is harboring these potent emotions, they are not freed up to function in relationships with others, and are not free to genuinely derive enjoyment from life. You probably know people just like this that are angry and bitter, or maybe that describes where you find yourself today. They are not pleasant to be around, and don't often put themselves around others any more than they have to. That is because their heart is walled off with emotional pain. The only way to free oneself from this emotional handicap is to work through the process of forgiveness, and to remove the emotional cast.

Don't Monkey Around With Forgiveness

As I mentioned previously in this chapter, I truly believe that a healthy dose of forgiveness could cure a lot of ills for many people who are dealing with dragging around the shackles of past hurts. For this reason I want to share with you a story that I came across in an adult Sunday school class at the First United Methodist Church in Wilmington, IL. The story has to do with a technique that trappers use in Asia to catch monkeys. The people who trap monkeys in this part of the world know that one thing that the monkeys really crave in their diet is salt. The trappers will take a hollow gourd and make a hole in the side of it just big enough for the monkey to stick its paw inside. Then they tie this gourd to a tree and place a block of salt inside of the gourd. The trap is set. When the monkey happens along and finds the gourd that has the salt block inside he reaches in to grab the prize. When he grabs onto the salt, however, his hand is too big to pull through the hole. Since the monkey refuses to "let go" he is trapped by his choice to "hold on". The monkey is then collected and sold.

We are much like the monkey who refuses to "let go" when we choose to "hold on" to past hurts and anger. We stay trapped in the very circumstances that we so much want to be rid of. Additionally, when you think about what we are holding on to that keeps us captive, we are actually allowing those who hurt us to have control over our emotional lives. I say this because unless you wake up in the morning hopeful that you find something to make you bitter and resentful, by choosing to cling to these toxic emotions you are empowering those whom you would least like to have control in your life. After the anger we feel at getting hurt exceeds its expiration date (the time at which we can actually do something to stop the hurt), it actually becomes harmful to us.

To close this very important topic, I wish to present a couple of thoughts. Once people begin to grasp the concept of what forgiveness is, and what it is not, I like to offer them another quality of forgiveness to consider. I suggest to them that forgiveness is not an event where we stand in judgment, slamming a gavel to proclaim that forgiveness is granted. Forgiveness is much more a lifestyle. It is routinely clearing out past hurts so that they do not accumulate in us, crushing us under their emotional weight. We should get into the habit of doing regular accounting of our emotional baggage, and be willing to let things go when appropriate. Finally, I want to present this thought on the topic of anger, "Anger is like an acid. It hurts the vessel that holds it much more than what it is poured out on (author unknown)."

8

Under Construction

Seeing that we are well into the internet generation, and knowing that some individuals reading this will have never known a world without the internet, it is a common experience to receive those random emails that contain some kind of life lesson in them. Most of the time when I read through these I immediately send them into the trash file. One of these emails that was forwarded to me not only caught my attention, but it has stuck with me ever since. I have no way of knowing whether it is an actual accounting of events or just email folklore, but the message is quite strong.

The setting is a college classroom on the first night of class. A philosophy professor steps in front of his class, and without saying a word, reaches behind his desk and pulls out a large jar. Then he reaches down and produces a box full of large rocks. Without saying a word, he proceeds to place the large rocks in the jar until it reaches the top of the jar. With this he asks the class if the jar is full, and they respond that it is. Then he reaches behind the desk and takes out a box that contains gravel. He scoops out some of the gravel and places it in the jar, shaking it occasionally, so that the gravel fills in around the large rocks. Then he again asks the class if the jar is full. They hesitate, trying to figure out where he is going with this demonstration, but eventually respond that the jar is indeed full. Next the professor produces a box filled with sand. He sprinkles the sand into the jar, shaking it occasionally, until the sand filled in around the gravel. The professor then asks again, "Is the jar full?" Not wanting to be wrong again, but also not seeing how anything else could fit in the jar, they again state that the jar is full. Finally, the professor reaches down and brings out a pitcher of water. He carefully pours the water into the jar and announces that the jar is now full. The point of this exercise was not to fool the students through trickery (although mission accomplished on that account), but rather he was trying to teach them an important lesson about life. You see, in order to fit everything into the jar that he did, he had to put the big things in first. Then everything else gets fit in around that. When you look at constructing a life, we should take this same approach. If we want an opportunity to be happy, we need to put the big things in first. For most people, the big rocks would be their spouse, their children, friends, or their relationship with God. The "gravel" in most people's lives would be their homes, their jobs, cars, and other such possessions. Important, but given the choice between the "big rocks" and the "gravel", the "big rocks" win every time. Everything else is the sand and the water. Electric bills, cutting the grass, changing the oil on the car, or painting the shutters are important, but in the grand scheme of things they are trumped by the "big rocks" and the "gravel". You see, if you put the sand and water in before the more important things, there is either not room for them or if you try to cram them in, it just makes for a big mess.

Many people who I see in my practice come to me literally exhausted from trying to get "everything" done in their lives, even though a person could not accomplish this if they had two lives to do it in. They chase their tails trying to do everything for everybody, the whole time neglecting their "big rocks". They present as the ideal example of the old adage of not confusing activity with productivity. These individuals are the embodiment of the Greek tragedy of Sisyphus. His punishment at the hands of the gods was to perpetually roll a marble block up a hill until it rolls back down just before he gets it to the top, then he has to start all over again . . . for eternity . . . active, but not productive.

What are the big rocks in your life? Are you placing them first, or are you allowing the things of lesser importance in your life squeeze them out? Alfred Adler was famous for his views on human behavior, and the difference between healthy living and unhealthy living. A phrase he would often state when he was trying to understand what motivates a person is "follow only movement". This literally means, "Listen to a person's behavior". Words are easy to say, but a person's actions will tell you where their heart really lies. If someone were to follow your movements for any period of time would they see that the words you say about what is important to you match your actions?

Now let's take a look at what really motivates people to act. People might seem like very complicated beings, and in some ways they are, but fundamentally what motivates all human behavior can be titrated down to one of two things. All human behavior is geared towards either getting us closer to what we desire in life, or it keeps us from what we are afraid of or wish to avoid. Every behavior from the most complex to the most simple is for one of these two reasons (or occasionally a combination of the two). When you examine the lives of many individuals who are plagued with depression, anxiety, and anger you will often find an individual where the scale of their life has tilted so that the preponderance of their choices are made to avoid that which they don't wish to deal. Therefore, when you look at what is controlling their lives, it is not really they that are in control, but rather that which they do not want to confront. Healthy people, on the other hand, will have most of their decisions made by moving towards what they want in life.

Once a person has this basic understanding of what motivates human behavior, it is important to find a vehicle to put this information to use. This is where I share with people the importance of having goals in life. I am not talking about goals like, "I want to be a millionaire by the time I am 29" (although if you can pull that one off, more power to you). I am talking about goals that are much more specific in nature. When it comes to charting a course for your life, you want to have both short-term and long-term goals for yourself. These two types of goals actually work with one another to bring about opportunities for success. Long-term goals help to give life direction as well as giving a person a means to chart the progress they are making towards achieving their goals. Short-term goals are the things that you put in place on a day-to-day basis to achieve your long-term goals. I want to steer around much of the pop psychology that is constantly being presented to people these days. It's not that the ideas presented in those theories are bad, it's just that most people do not put them to practical use. I myself have attended many of these talks. I have been told to write down goals on a piece of paper and then put it in my sock drawer so that I come across them regularly. I found that piece of paper the last time that I moved. Another well-meaning speaker encouraged the audience to make good use of every second. She said that we should use the time we have while we let our dog out to do his "business" to organize our spice rack. With that I stopped listening. The ideas that most motivational speakers relay are not really new. Most say the same exact things with new terminology. I want to present the ideas of setting goals for your life, not in the "new best way", but rather in a practical, meaningful way that is portable and user friendly.

First, let's tackle long-term goals. We start with these because they actually form the foundation on which we will construct our short-term goals. Long-term goals actually come in a variety of forms. Regardless, long-term goals tell you where you want to end up in a certain part of your life, what you ultimately want that facet of your life to look like. I will often refer to these as the "als" of your life, because most of them will end in "al". Some of the facets to consider in developing long-term goals for yourself are as follows: relational, occupational, social, recreational, spiritual, parental, financial, and physical. Depending on your life's circumstances there may be others, but I think you get the idea. Think about all of these different long-term goals coming together as a mosaic, pieced together to ultimately form the life that you want to have. Many of these goals will overlap and/or influence one another. Take for example; your long-term recreational goal is to be involved in competitive yachting. Well, your occupational and financial goals need to be ones that will support the financial need to participate in that activity. Determining what these long-term goals will be in your life requires a lot of deep consideration on your part. The goals that you come up with should reflect your priorities and values in life. They should also be personally meaningful to you. I could suggest to a person who is developing a long-term occupational goal for themselves that they should be an accountant or a chemist because those are good jobs. However, if that individual does not like math or science they are not good goals for them.

Short-term goals are the pieces that you put in place to achieve your long-term goals. Survivalists will tell you that if you are lost in the forest there is one approach that will help you to get out. This same logic applies to how we successfully navigate our lives. The strategy involves picking a point in the distance and then walking towards it. That point may be a mountain or some other structure, but it should be something that you can keep your eyes fixed on. As you set off on your endeavor to get to this point you may find obstacles like rocks, trees, water and such, but if you continue to work your way towards your target eventually you will arrive. That point in the distance is your long-term goal. The steps that you take to get there are your short-term goals. Many years ago I set an educational goal for myself. I wanted to earn a bachelor's degree. Prior to starting my freshman year I saw that I needed to accumulate at least 128 credit hours to earn a degree. That is a daunting task when you are sitting there with zero. I looked at my major and the classes that were required to earn my degree. As I took the various classes and completed them I would cross them off. With a glimpse I could see where I was at in the process and what I needed to focus on next to achieve my goal. Eventually I earned my degree, and then a master's degree, and eventually passed my state's licensing exam. By accomplishing these educational goals I was able to also accomplish my occupational goal of becoming a therapist. Short-term goals also help people to make healthy decisions in their lives. Let's take a look at this in action.

We will take for example a high school student who is deciding on a career path. We will call him Greg for the sake of example. Greg decides that he is really interested in the medical arts and would like to become a physician (long-term goal). Understanding that to accomplish this goal he must go to college and then be accepted to medical school, he has to choose a school that will put him in a good position to be successful. To select an undergraduate school, he must consider that medical schools are very selective. He must select a school with a strong academic reputation rather than the best fraternity life (short-term goal). He also must select a major that will prepare him for his entrance exams for medical school (short-term goal). Once he is in college he will face many more options for developing short-term goals. He will need to consider what clubs and experiences will make him a more desirable candidate for medical school (short-term goal). He will also need to make other choices like whether he should go out drinking with friends tonight or to prepare for his biology exam tomorrow (short-term goal). By stacking series of these short-term goals one upon another, Greg will eventually put himself in a position to be successful in pursuing his long-term goal of being a doctor. Again, there are no guarantees that this will always be successful, but one can certainly guarantee a lack of success by being active, but not productive. Greg, by the way, will eventually go on to become a doctor, and will be the head of the Diagnostic Medicine Department at Princeton-Plainsboro Teaching Hospital.

Before we conclude this section about what motivates behavior and drives a person's decisions, I want to discuss what is behind problematic behaviors that people demonstrate.

Previously in this chapter we have explored how all behavior is motivated by moving towards what we desire or away from that which scares us or is unpleasant. I have encouraged the reader to adopt a "moving towards" approach to creating goals for their lives. Many people, however, will adopt troubling or problematic patterns of behavior that are not healthy for the individual at all. In trying to understand these behaviors and what motivates them, we will run them through a process to ascertain the answer. First, we can eliminate the possibility that the troubling behavior gets the person closer to what they want in life. The very nature of the troubling behavior allows us to do this. By default, it means that the behavior helps the person to avoid something they are afraid of or that which they do not wish to deal. At this point the answer should become clearer. If not, ask yourself this question, "by continuing to engage in this behavior what is it that I am not able to do?" A more detailed series of open-ended questions Adlerian therapists will ask their clients will typically bring the answer to the surface. These questions asked in this order are as follows:

1. The worst part about [insert problem behavior here] is . . .
2. If there is anything good about [problem behavior] it just might be . . .
3. In a strange, that I have never really thought of before, [problem behavior] just might protect me from . . .

Usually by the time you get through these three statements the answer is fairly clear.

Often, just having knowledge of the behavior is not enough to correct it. Helping someone to understand their poor behavior, or private logic, will make it less "rewarding", but will not stop it all together. At this point, when I am working with clients, they will say, "Ok, I get it, but I still don't know what I should do." The oddity of this situation that I point out to people is that most of the time they do know what they should do, they just don't allow themselves to access that part of them that possesses good advice. When they protest that they really don't know what to do I ask them this simple question, "What would you tell your best friend to do if they were in the same exact situation that you are in?" Now they smile, realizing that the right answer has just presented itself. You see, most of us inherently know healthy from unhealthy, we just choose to avoid applying it to our own lives. When we look at it in the third person, the problem is a lot easier to solve. That, as I point out to my clients, is why I got into the field of psychotherapy. Other people's problems are a lot easier to solve than our own!

9

The Prodigal

I n my private practice, at any given time, roughly 40% of my caseload is made up of couples seeking help with their relationships. Add to that the many individuals that I work with who are dealing with troubled relationships as at least part of the challenge that they are facing and it is pretty clear that this relationship thing is a tough deal! Divorce statistics are staggering. While numbers fluctuate from survey to survey, a survey out some time ago said that 50% of first marriages fail, 60% of second marriages fail, and 70% of third marriages fail. Those are staggering numbers, and if you add to that all of those who are impacted by divorce such as children, relatives, and friends, and you are approaching a situation of catastrophic proportions.

In this chapter I want to talk about information that I provide to individuals who seek assistance with troubled relationships. In the next chapter I will share many of the strategies that I find helpful in dealing with couples.

There is a model that I follow that holds age-old wisdom for individuals who are trying to deal with challenging relationships. It is a parable from the Book of Luke (Luke 15:11-32) that is commonly known as The Parable of The Prodigal Son. Spiritually, when Jesus relayed this story He was talking about lost souls, but He was also providing people a roadmap for how to approach individuals who are experiencing trouble in relationships.

Briefly, the story is about a wealthy land owner who has two sons. One of the sons is hard working and causes the father not a single concern. The other is like an unbridled colt that seeks immediate gratification and is all about himself. One day the wilder of the two approaches his father with a proposition. He explains to his father that it is quite obvious that one day the father will die, and when that happens, the sons will divide what the father has for their inheritance. The wide-eyed son asks to cut to the chase. He asks his father to give him his share now, even though the father is still among the living, so that he can go about the process of enjoying his half while he is young. This, of course, is a tremendous insult to the father and he had every right to send him on his way with nothing. However, the father grants his son's short-sighted wish and turns over half of his fortune. Well, the son wastes little time in enjoying the wealth. He spends it on wine, women, gambling, and various other indulgences with little concern for the long-term. In relatively short order, the son finds himself penniless. He is broke, in a foreign land, with no way of knowing from where his next meal was coming. Devastated and desperate, the son is forced to take a job feeding swine (and if you know anything about the Jewish faith, it doesn't get any worse than that). He actually begins to envy the pigs he is feeding since at least they have food. At this moment he experiences a revelation. He thinks back to his days living at home. He realizes that the men who work for his father have a life far superior to what he is currently living, so he humbles himself and begins the long journey back home. When he gets there he plans to ask his father to hire him on to work his land. Broken and dispirited the son approaches the road that his father lives on. From a distance the father sees him and runs to him. As he does, he shouts to his staff to get a robe for his son and to place rings on his fingers, because his son who was lost is now home. A celebration is planned and all seems well (except for the dutiful son who is, shall we say, less than thrilled with the events).

You see, within the confines of this simple story are all the tools that one needs to deal with wayward relationships. Let's take a look at the players in this story. First, there is the prodigal. This individual has wandered off the path and is headed for no good. Quite obviously, he is not receptive to the counsel of others. The father and many others in this story have no doubt attempted to show the son the error of his ways to no avail. He (the son) knows it all and has it all figured out. This is not usually the one who is seeking help in my office or reading books such as this. The one exception to this is the individual who is being forced into counseling by the courts or their family. That almost never goes anywhere productive. They seem bound and determined not only to run the car into the ditch, but to light it on fire as well. This may be the spouse who "loves you, but is not sure they are *in love* with you", the child who is hanging with the wrong crowd and making poor choices, the sibling who seems to turn on you, or the friend or co-worker who seems to be pouring their life down the drain. In other words, they are the person who is the object of the problem.

The second player in the story is the father. Now here is where the wisdom lies. Let's look carefully at how the father responds. First, he doesn't try to stop his son. Even though the father knows that it is a poor choice, he does not try to roadblock him. I want to clarify at this time that in this instance I am speaking about dealing with an adult who legally has the right to make certain decisions. Parents dealing with minor children have a responsibility to protect themselves from themselves at times. Dealing with minor children brings up a whole host of concerns that go beyond the scope of this book. Back to the case at hand, the father allows his son to make the decision knowing that along with that will eventually come the consequences associated with his choices. This is not a situation in which the son is ignorant of what the healthy choice is. If a person is making a poor decision based on lack of knowledge, then you can certainly educate them and, in this case, they should be receptive to good counsel. I am talking about the situation where the person has been informed and the matter has been discussed, yet they still wish to head down a dangerous path. As painful as it might seem (and it definitely is painful) you have little choice but to allow the person to learn from their mistakes.

This actually goes along with the ideas of boundaries and locus of control that were previously discussed in this book. Remember, the father in this story can only control his own thoughts, feelings, and behavior. Trying to control what his son was intent on doing would have failed miserably. Truth be told, the son in this story would have found a way to do what he wanted regardless of what the father said.

Further, let's look at how the father handles the son's ongoing poor behavior. He does not intervene. By all indications he certainly possessed the wealth to send people after his son to hog-tie him and drag him back kicking and screaming. What would this have accomplished? It's not like the son would be brought back against his will and all of a sudden he would have an epiphany of the error of his ways. He had to be allowed to learn from the natural consequences of his behavior. It is only at this time that a person can genuinely humble themselves and seek to create a healthy relationship. And now a cold hard truth, not every story in real life ends with a joyous reunion. Sometimes the prodigal does not return. Sometimes they face dire consequences and continue on their ill-fated paths. In some cases (such as continuing in a drug or alcohol consumed life) it means bringing about their own demise.

There are also situations in which the estranged individual(s) remain toxic to the person struggling to come to grips with lost relationship. Under these circumstances, the grief and sadness associated with the loss are more associated with the person(s) that you want that them to be rather than who they have been and really are. To sever ties and keep distance from these individuals is the wise thing to do, as the only outcome of associating with them is distress. This is where groups such as Al-Anon can be helpful in providing strength to family members.

If the father does not actively try to corral his son, what does he do? He maintains openness. He never disowns the son or slams the door shut on the relationship. The father has clear expectations of his son, and what it would take to recreate a healthy relationship with his son. He waits with arms open for the son to return, not under any circumstances, but under healthy circumstances. This can be very difficult for people in the role of the "father" to accept because it feels like doing nothing. One has to ask themselves in this situation, "What are the alternatives?" In most situations it's not that you haven't said things. The "son" is choosing not to listen. Until that individual is in a place where they are receptive to a healthier reality, patience is your key instrument. For many, faith and prayer can be solid companions to help get you through these trying times.

Lastly, there is the oft forgotten member of this story, the other brother who has done things the right way. In the actual parable the lesson to be learned is that established Christians should not be resentful towards those who take a while to come around to faith. Life lesson-wise, it is helpful for the person in the "father" role to understand that spouses, siblings, relatives, and friends who may be negatively impacted by the behavior of a prodigal (either through financial resources or extra attention diverted towards the prodigal) may be very resentful. They are truly hurt by these situations, and it is important to be understanding of the role that they play and to validate the feelings that they experience. Regardless, if you are finding yourself in a situation such as this, know that it is heart-wrenchingly painful. Also understand that situations such as these call for extreme attention to healthy boundaries, and that maintaining a patient openness does not equate to doing nothing. It is simply dealing with the realities of the situation at hand.

10
Just A Couple Things

As I have mentioned previously, I see a significant number of couples in my private practice. Some therapists find couples work draining, and for that reason avoid working with them all together. While I do find working with couples quite a challenge clinically, I also find this work incredibly rewarding. To see a couple move from a place of being bitter and angry with their spouse and fed up with the relationship in general move to a place of being able to reconnect and to be loving to the other is nothing short of a miracle to behold.

What has helped me to develop my approach to couples work is the education that I have received through reading some of the great minds in the field of relationships. In this chapter I want to introduce some of these works as well as my take on some of the most significant material that the authors present in their various works. This is not meant to be a summation of the entire works sited, but rather an abstraction of material from these authors that I have compiled to develop my model for working with couples. I strongly encourage you to read these works for yourself if you want to understand the entirety of the theories in the author's own words. As I explain to couples I meet with on the first session, I will help them to sample from the therapy buffet. Then we will go back and spend more time on the material that is pertinent to their particular situation. The books that I will discuss are in no particular order. As I review each I will point out how I incorporate the material into my model of what a healthy relationship should look and function like.

A book that I will typically start out discussing is a wonderful work written by Emerson Eggerichs entitled, *Love & Respect*. In this book Eggerichs undertakes a detailed exploration of what men and women need from a marriage. He ultimately determines that men and women have very different needs in relationships. For women, the overriding need in a relationship is to feel loved by her partner. And for men, what is most important in intimate relationships is to feel respected. Admittedly, when you really stop to examine what goes into loving someone and being respectful towards them there is a lot of overlap, but there are some important differences. Eggerichs goes on to discuss in great detail what a man must do to be loving towards his wife and what a woman must do to be respectful towards her husband. He actually devotes several chapters to each, creating the acronyms CHAIRS and COUPLE to be reminders for the various ingredients for each. When I use this material I carve off what I find to really capture the essence of love and respect.

For husbands, I tell them that if they want to have a healthy relationship they must be loving to their wife. I tell them that if they can focus on creating a marital environment that has three key elements they can have a significant impact on the quality of their relationship. For a man to be loving towards his wife he must make her feel special in his life, she needs to feel cared for in ways that are meaningful to her, and she needs to feel protected physically and emotionally. Now let's take a closer look at each of these.

To help a wife to feel special in his world, a husband must create a place for her that is reserved just for her. It should be not just any old place, but the best place in his life. Nothing (work, hobbies, play, etc.) and no one (friends, family, even children) should infringe on this place in his life. She needs to see through his actions that she has priority status in his life. This is actually supported in the wedding vows that couples make on their wedding day. While they vary to some degree there is always a statement made where it is said that he will love, <u>honor</u>, and cherish his wife for all the days of his life.

The second part of being loving towards a wife is to demonstrate caring in a way that is meaningful to her. This means that the husband needs to find ways that are meaningful to his wife and not just what is most convenient or familiar to the husband. You see, when we take the time to really understand our partners we show them the value that they hold in our lives. Bringing home flowers on Friday may be a very nice gesture for a husband to make, but if his wife is looking for spending some quality time with him, flowers will not be an adequate substitute for having him there. To learn what your partner wants in the way of being cared for, a man must do some detective work. Talk to her friends if you don't know what she is interested in. Pay attention to what she reads, what she looks at in the newspaper, what she watches on TV, and oh yeah . . . . listen to what she says herself. Also, a wonderful resource is a book we will discuss shortly entitled *Five Love Languages* by Gary Chapman.

Lastly, a woman has to feel protected by her husband. This is both physically and emotionally. Physically a husband should be tender towards his wife. There should never even be the threat of physical harm. If physical abuse is a part of your relationship, put this book down and immediately get yourself into therapy. If you are a woman who has suffered from physical abuse at the hands of your husband you have to take immediate action to stop this cycle whether your relationship survives or not. Another part of feeling safe physically is the husband's duty to provide for his wife and family. I am not talking lavish gifts, but a secure home environment with the basic needs being met. This may seem kind of dated in its logic, but believe me it is an important part of a healthy relationship. Emotionally, helping a woman to feel protected is a bit more challenging for many men. It means avoiding being critical, not yelling or name calling, and not being intentionally cruel to her. It means understanding your wife well enough that you avoid saying things that she would take as hurtful or insensitive, even if you do not intend them to be. It means supporting the wife through various struggles that she has with her day and with other people. Even if a husband does not agree with his wife, he should support her right to have her own beliefs and opinions in these matters. Being able to create an environment where a wife feels special, cared for, and protected will foster a sense of feeling loved by her husband.

For wives, it is important to extend respect to her husband. This can sometimes be a challenge, especially in relationships that have been in turmoil. Oft times it seems hard for a wife to find much at all that she respects in her husband if the relationship has been sour for any length of time. Also, women will have to deal with the belief that respect is something that must be earned. That may seem logical in most situations, but if a woman is looking to get some positive momentum going in her relationship she will have to find ways of demonstrating respect. The three elements of respect that I encourage women to focus on extending to their husbands are to help him to feel appreciated, acknowledge his efforts at work and around the house, and acknowledge his good qualities, not just to him, but also to others that she speaks to.

Yes, it is true that the male ego does require care and attention. Men have to feel appreciated by their spouses. This is a need that probably dates back to childhood where he was told that he was a good boy for doing this or that. Men may grow in stature, but that desire to feel appreciated by others, a wife in particular, never goes away.

Closely related to feeling appreciated is having his efforts be acknowledged as being important. Even if the efforts that a husband puts forth around the house might seem minimal to a wife in a given relationship, it is still important to acknowledge any helpful of thoughtful things that he does. If it involves fixing something, cleaning something, or even just picking up after himself take time to acknowledge it. Some women may feel that it is over-the-top to do this since they don't get pats on the back for all they do (even though they are deserved). But let's remember the behavioral technique of shaping. This involves offering reinforcers to someone for getting closer and closer to a desired behavior. You start out with the original behavior and selectively reinforce the desired behavior until you see more and more of it. Just think of it. If a wife wants a husband to help out more around the house is it more likely to happen with a "Thanks for taking that glass into the kitchen," or a "Take that glass to the sink. I am not your mother!"?

Lastly, it is very important for women to point out what they admire about their husbands, and not just to their husbands, but to others as well. When a woman talks up what she likes about her husband it helps him to feel positive about himself, his relationship, and his wife. Men thrive on this sort of reinforcement. Conversely, nothing can diminish a man's interest in working on a relationship more than a critical wife. Men tend to be very functional in their approaches to things. If a man experiences his wife as being harsh and critical it will be hard for him to make a case for wanting to get closer to her.

Eggerichs points out that when love and respect are not present in a marriage it leads to something he calls the *crazy cycle*. Here the couple just keeps digging deeper and deeper into the marital abyss. The way out of it is for each partner to work on meeting their partner's need, either love or respect, unconditionally. This is called the *energizing cycle*. That means no strings attached, non-contingently, no "I'll do this if you do that". If you can approach your relationship this way and maintain it you improve the viability of your relationship and feeling fulfilled.

Another author whom I frequently reference when discussing the elements that go into creating a healthy relationship is Gary Smalley. Smalley is the author of several great works in the area of relationships ("Love Is A Decision", "Secrets To Lasting Love", and "If Only He Knew" to name a few). I find that Smalley's work in the area of communication is something that couples easily relate to. He states that there are actually five different levels of communication in an intimate relationship. The first level is "cliché". This is the "Hi, how are you?" kind of statements that we make to people we see in the grocery store. The second level of communication is "functional". This is the type of communication that we use to accomplish things. With functional communication we can pay the bills, cut the grass, do the laundry, and decide who is going to pick up the kids from school. Many couples spend the majority of their time in functional communication because it is effective in getting things done. The problem is that "cliché" and "functional" forms of communications do not involve actual relating to one another. We could use these with someone with whom we are just cohabitating. Real relating doesn't begin until we actually reach the third level, "thoughts/opinions". This is where we actually begin sharing of ourselves, and what we really think about things. This does not mean just being able to share our safe thoughts, it means being able to share all of our thoughts, positive or negative. The fourth level is our "feelings". This is one that husbands usually love to talk about (about as much as removing one's own appendix with that butter knife). Again, like thoughts, it's not just the safe feelings, but all the feelings, good and bad. The deepest level of communication in an intimate relationship is "needs". In other words, what is it that we need from this relationship in particular to feel satisfied? Just to clarify, we all have needs in our relationships. That does not make us "needy" in the relationship. The fact that we pick out one person with whom to form this kind of intimate relationship with means that we are willing to make ourselves vulnerable (risk) so that we can experience satisfaction (reward).

The ranking of these levels of communication has to do with how vulnerable we must make ourselves to share that type of material. "How is your day going?" is a lot different from saying, "I really need your support in this." As was previously discussed in this book, in order to be happy a person must be willing to take risk. Therefore it is incumbent on both parties to create a safe environment within which to share the intimate details of thoughts, feelings, and needs. If a person does not feel safe enough to share then you end up spending a lot of time talking about topics like milk and ketchup. These are also people who will report feeling lonely in their relationship. And anyone who has experienced it will tell you that it is more painful to be lonely in a relationship than to be lonely by yourself. It is this kind of limitation in communication that leaves relationships vulnerable to affairs. If people are not sharing their thoughts, feelings, and needs it allows them to create separate existences for themselves. They will have their "family life" with the spouse and children and then they will have the "affair life" where they are getting romantic needs met. In my 23 years of counseling I have never worked with a couple on the topic of infidelity who also stated that they had healthy communication in these deeper levels.

In order to create a safe environment to share on these deeper levels there are certain things that must be guarded against. Criticism, defensiveness, sarcasm, judgment, and being dismissive are sure ways of compromising security in communication. Even if there is material on which a couple disagrees, they can still work towards understanding each other. That is often a much more attainable goal that trying to always agree with each other. Couples who are able to create an environment that affords them the opportunity to share on these deeper levels report significantly more satisfaction from their marital relationship.

John Gottman is one of this country's foremost authorities on relationships. His method of understanding not just what creates problems in relationships, but also what makes them thrive is beyond reproach. During the first session with a new couple I undoubtedly will share with them some of the true gems from his classic work, *The Seven Principles For Making Marriage Work*. Three elements of his theory that I find particularly pertinent to most couples are the four horsemen of the apocalypse, flooding, and the balance of positive and negative sentiment.

First there are what Gottman refers to as the "four horsemen of the apocalypse" of relationships, or in other words, four things that when they show up in your relationship, damage is being done. The first of the horsemen is criticism. Criticism is when you have an issue with a person and you attack the person rather than dealing with the behavior. Let's take for example a person who leaves a towel on the bathroom floor. A criticism might look like this . . . "I can't believe how lazy you are. You never think of anyone but yourself!" Try to think about a productive response that a person could possibly have to being attacked in this manner. There is not a healthy way to respond to this. A much healthier approach, as described by Gottman, is to issue a complaint. A complaint deals with the behavior rather than attacking the person. A complaint might come in the form of, "You left a towel on the floor again. You know we have talked about this and you know how it leaves me feeling when it happens." This gives you room to work with each other. The second horsemen is defensiveness. This comes in the form of, "Oh yeah, well how about you??!" When criticism and defensiveness get going there is little chance that anything good will come of it. As a matter of fact, criticism and defensiveness will often lead to the third horsemen, contempt. Contempt is when a person is fed up and disgusted with a situation or with another person. It will manifest itself in the form of saying hurtful things, doing hurtful things, yelling, name calling, or sometimes threatening. Of all the four horsemen, contempt is often the most damaging. Hurtful things said or done in the heat of battle can be apologized for, but they cannot be unsaid or undone. Contempt will often leave the most painful emotional scars. The last of the four horsemen is stonewalling. This is something that is more often employed by men, but women are capable of using it as well. It is when a person is physically present, but they withdraw themselves emotionally. In a way, they punish the person by withholding their affections. It will frequently show up as short, dismissive comments like, "Fine", "Whatever", etc. Regardless, it is important that couples be aware of these four destructive forces, and to work on minimizing their presence in their relationship.

Flooding, when it comes to relationships, is not something that you need to roll your pants up to deal with. Rather it has to do with what happens when a basic human reaction to threat shows up during conflict in a relationship. The system in question is a part of our brain called the sympathetic nervous system, in particular our fight or flight mechanism. This is the part of our brain that constantly surveys our environment for any type of physical threat. When it perceives a threat, it activates and prepares us to fight what is attacking us or to take flight and get the heck out of there. This system is very helpful if a dog starts chasing after you. As was previously mentioned, you get a shot of adrenaline, your heart rate increases, your breathing quickens, your blood pressure rises, and blood gets directed to your large muscle groups. This is perfect if you are preparing to fight an attacker or to make tracks and get out of there. Another physiological change that occurs when this system is activated is that our thinking changes. It changes from being able to consider a wide variety of options to just being able to think about one thing. This is actually adaptive if a dog is chasing you because you do not have time to consider seven different options. You really want to think about what you are going to do and do it! Our sympathetic nervous system, being rather primitive, is not able to differentiate between a physical threat (like a dog) and an emotional threat (something hurtful our partner says). So if we are dealing with a conflict and something hurtful gets said, your heart rate will go up, your breathing will quicken, and all the rest. This includes your thinking being limited to thinking about one thing, and one thing only. Believe me, having worked with couples for almost a quarter of a century, that one thing the "flooded" spouse is thinking about is not, "Boy, they are making some really good points right now." It's more likely, "Why don't you leave me alone?", or "Why aren't you listening to me?", or "Why don't you just shut up?!"

When flooding has occurred with one or both parties involved in a conflict, there is really only one thing that can happen to cut your losses. The couple has to enact a two-step process. First, they have to agree, in advance of the fight, that when things reach a certain point (flooding), they both agree to adhere to a time-out.

This can be called by either person, and they both have to allow it. This stops further damage, such as contempt, from occurring. Secondly, they have to agree to return to the discussion (preferably within twenty-four hours). And since it takes at least twenty-five minutes after being removed from the triggering incident to turn off all of the physiological effects, it's probably safe to wait at least one hour before trying to resume a conversation on the challenging issue.

Another facet of Gottman's theory that I share with couples on the first or second session is his concept of positive and negative sentiment. In general terms, this speaks to the balance of positive and negative things that exist in the relationship at any given time. In the early days of a relationship, when the couple is still in what is referred to as the infatuation stage, there is an abundance of positive things going on in the relationship. That other person is so wonderful they can seem to do no wrong. However, when the couple moves into the reality phase of their relationship she begins to wonder if he needs a GPS to locate the clothes hamper and he is mystified by the fact that she cannot remember that after three thousand miles the car would sure appreciate an oil change. If this kind of negativity gets legs and begins to grow the couple may be headed for "negative sentiment override". This is the term Gottman uses when the balance of positive to negative elements in the relationship tips towards negative. As we have previously discussed, when we choose to entertain negative thoughts about a person we also welcome in the negative emotions that come with them. This creates a toxic environment for relationships and if it is not kept in check, it can bring about the relationship's ultimate demise.

The remedy for negative sentiment is actually fairly simple (again, simple does not always equate with easy). Each member of the couple has to work on taking control of their thoughts. By doing this the challenge comes down to catching your partner doing something right. Believe it or not, each of you probably does numerous things "right" throughout the day. They just go unnoticed or they get overshadowed with the things that are wrong. The following story illustrates this point.

There was once a king who had two of his knights called before him. He informed each of them that he had a very important task for them to complete. He looked to the knight on his left and told him, "Over the next thirty days I want you to go throughout my kingdom, every square inch, and document for me every weed that you find. I want every last detail there is to know about each and every weed." To the knight on his right he stated, "And for you, I want you to go throughout my kingdom over the next thirty days and document every flower that you can find. I want every detail there is to know about all the flowers in my land." Each knight set about his task and at the end of thirty days they were brought before the king to provide their report. The first knight approaches the king and states with confidence, "King, I am amazed at what I have found. I have learned that every square inch of your kingdom is filled with weeds. They are of every shape and size, but one thing is sure, they fill your entire kingdom." The king looks to the second knight who approaches. The second knight states with equal confidence, "King, I also was amazed at what I found. I learned that every square inch of your land is filled with flowers of every shape and color." Now neither of the knights was being untruthful, they were just demonstrating a common human phenomenon. In life, whatever you go out looking for is what you will find. Therefore, if you really look for the positive qualities of your mate, positive qualities will be exactly what you will find. Additionally, you will also be welcoming in the positive feelings associated with those thoughts.

Gottman's research indicates a ratio that exists in healthy relationships of five positive comments for every negative one. It is fairly simple to imagine that if you are getting five positives from someone for every negative that that is something that pulls people together. Conversely, if you are getting many more negatives than positives, that is something that pushes people apart. This is actually one of the most simple and effective ways to turn a relationship around and get it moving into a healthy direction.

David Richo is the author of *How To Be An Adult In Relationships*. This book, which draws from the psychological theories of Carl Jung, offers a simple way of understanding some basic necessities of healthy adult relationships. One of the aspects of Richo's work that I find particularly helpful in explaining to couples some of the basics they need to have a healthy relationship is called "the five A's in healthy relationships". In other words, these are five things that must be present in a relationship between adults if it is going to be healthy. The five A's are *acceptance, allowing, attention, appreciation,* and *affection.* Of these five, I have found that two of them seem to be more challenging than the other three for couples to master. Those two are acceptance and allowing.

To clarify, acceptance does not mean that a person just has to accept whatever another person wants to send their way. What acceptance is about is more about what we are willing and/or able to accept from the other. Think of it this way, all of us draw lines in the sand regarding what is acceptable to us and what is not. As long as everything in our relationship with another person is on the acceptable side of the line, we can have a healthy relationship with that person. To clarify, that does not mean that we are thrilled with everything, it just means that we are willing to live with it. If, however, there is something(s) that exists that is unacceptable to us, it guarantees that we cannot have a healthy relationship with that person. At the very best we can have a functional relationship, but the relationship will not be able to gain much depth at all. If this condition exists there are really two things that can occur to address it. One is that the behavior of the other must change in order to make it acceptable (i.e. the lying must stop, infidelity must end, drug-taking behavior must cease), and the other is that the person who finds the behavior unacceptable can move the line of acceptability. The latter of the two should be closely scrutinized before it occurs. The reason is that once a person begins moving the line of acceptability they open themselves up to potentially toxic relationships. It is always good to consult with a therapist, clergy member, or trusted friend or family member before you begin to accept something that you previously found unacceptable.

The second "A" that is challenging to relationships is allowing. Allowing means that each person in the relationship allows the other to be who they are with no strings attached. They are allowed to have their own thoughts, feelings, and behaviors, and even if there are differences there will not be punishments or negative consequences for the person who holds them. As we have mentioned previously, healthy relationships do not require two people who agree on everything. That is not likely to happen, and if it did, it would probably be pretty boring. What it means is that a person should not have to fundamentally change who they are in order to maintain a relationship. Once acceptance and allowing have been achieved, attention, appreciation, and affection will often flow naturally.

The last work that I will detail, and one that I share with most of the couples with whom I work, is *Five Love Languages*, by Gary Chapman. In this well-known work, Chapman explores the five ways that humans look for and demonstrate love to one another. The five love languages are (in no particular order), *tokens, acts of service, words, quality time, and physical touch.* Tokens are just that, simple items that relay the message that I know what you like and I think about you even when you are not around. Tokens can be a card under a windshield wiper, a favorite candy, a scented candle, or flowers just to mention a few. Acts of service involve doing something nice for the other person. This might be picking up a household chore their partner usually does when their partner is busy or stressed, washing their car without being asked, or perhaps making them their favorite meal. Words involves telling another person how you feel about them, either through a simple statement or well thought out prose. Quality time involves time set aside for just the two of you. There should be no TV, cellphones, kids, or other distractions to detract from the attention you are offering to each other. This might be going for a walk, sitting on the deck, going out for dinner, or even a weekend getaway. However it turns out, the time must be spent with focused attention on each other and the relationship. Lastly, there is physical touch. This can come in the form of pats on the back, hugs, kisses, holding hands, or intercourse. Even though all of these might sound very appealing, each of us has a preferred love language. This is essential information for partners to know about each other. All too often I talk with couples about this and they are surprised by their partner's love language. They have been providing tokens regularly and thinking they are doing a bang-up job when their partner really desires quality time.

The works that I have cited here and briefly described are part of what I refer to as my couples' buffet. I provide the couple with a short introduction to these works in the first session or two and then we go back for a larger "portion" later on based on the particular needs of their relationship. Additionally, there are many more resources out there that are excellent resources for couples who are dealing with relationship concerns. I strongly recommend "Relationship Rescue" by Dr. Phil McGraw and "Courtship After Marriage" by Zig Ziglar. Additionally, two movies that I will suggest to couples are "Fireproof" and "The Story Of Us", both of which contain material that is of tremendous benefit to couples who find ways of understanding the material and incorporating it into their relationship.

11
Did Ya Hear The One About...?

I n the world of mental health humor is often the forgotten
family member. This no doubt has to do with the nature
of the pain and hurt experienced by those whose lives are
in chaos and turmoil. I know from my own personal experience
in the field of counseling that the strife those individuals bear
needs to be dealt with in a very sensitive manner. I also know
that there is a risk that a person can become consumed by these
issues. When you consider what we have discussed earlier in
this book, entertaining persistent thoughts about hurtful issues
will also invite the potentially debilitating emotions that are
associated with them. Therefore, it can be very therapeutic for a
person to take respite from these concerns, to allow themselves
an emotional breather if you will. When I was working at the
day hospital at Riverside Medical Center, we dealt with some
of the most extreme emotional conditions one could imagine.
Even though the group therapy sessions could be intense and
emotionally draining, I always ended the groups with a joke of
some sort. By doing this it seemed to bring a natural break from
the issue at hand, allowing those who participated in the group

and myself to transition back to the lighter side of life. It allowed the individual who is dealing with this burden to place it back on the shelf for a while, not as a means of denial, but rather as a way of reallocating their emotional resources to address the demands of life at hand. The issues requiring attention are not going anywhere. I have found that it is much more empowering for an individual to realize that they can deal with these concerns on their time rather than waiting for the issue to pounce on them at an inopportune time.

Another therapeutic benefit to humor is that it is actually good for you. Researchers have determined that a good sound belly laugh will help to release endorphins into the bloodstream. These chemicals are pleasure producers and can actually help a person to deal more effectively with pain, both emotional and physical. Another fact about humor is its relation to reality. The best comedians know that the funniest jokes are those that contain pure, unbridled reality. When you hear the content of the joke it immediately registers with you and you can relate. It is also understood that the type of humor that a person relates to and enjoys has a lot to do with their personality. If someone tells you a joke and you cannot relate to it, it will not resonate with you and will fail to tickle your funny bone.

In years gone by, racial, religious, and ethnic humor was common. These were often born out of the social issues of the time. Jokes about politicians, lawyers, and especially male/female relationships persist because of the enduring nature of these experiences (even if transient and/or temporary) in people's lives. Let's take a brief look at some jokes and see why we find them funny and how they can actually be put to some therapeutic use.

Saul was a devoutly religious man who was always trying to do "good" for others. He also wanted very little in return. In fact, throughout his entire adult life he only prayed for one thing . . . he wanted to win the lottery. Day after day he would perform these acts of kindness without looking for reciprocations. When he would pray, he would note prayers for all of the individuals that he had encountered that day, as well as friends and family, but nothing for himself until he would end the prayer, "Lord, please, just once, let me win the lottery." As the years go by, age catches up with Saul and he takes ill. Still he prays for the needs of others until he ends the prayer with, "Lord, please, just once, let me with the lottery." Eventually Saul passes away and he finds himself standing in front of God who is welcoming him into heaven. He looks up at God and says, "Lord, I was your faithful servant for my whole life. I helped countless people and never asked for anything in return. Throughout my entire existence I only prayed for one thing and you would never grant it. Why, oh Lord, would you never . . . not once . . . ever let me win the lottery?" God looks kindly down at his faithful son and says, "Saul, you still needed to buy a ticket."

Some people that I counsel enter therapy with a sort of "victim" mentality. They talk about all of the inequities in life, and how others seem to get all the breaks, but they get none. What these individuals seem to miss is that most successful and prosperous individuals did not get "lucky" with their good fortune, they made it happen or at least put them into a position to have good fortune. In this joke, God would have been more than willing to let Saul win the lottery, but he never bought a ticket. He had to put himself into a position to be successful.

Late one night Mike was walking down the sidewalk when he came up to a streetlight. Under the streetlight was a friend of Mike's, Tom. Tom was down on all fours feeling around in the grass. Mike sees him and asks Tom what he is doing. Tom says, "I am looking for my keys." Not being in much of a hurry this time of night, Mike decides to help his friend locate his keys and asks him where exactly he lost them. Tom points to a place about 15 yards away from the streetlight and says, "I lost them over there." Mike quizzically looks at his friend and says, "If you lost them over there, why are you looking over here?" Tom looks at Mike and matter-of-factly says, "The light is better over here."

Again, it is common for people who are challenged in their lives to look for answers outside of themselves. "I am this way because my parents treated me poorly", "People like me don't have a chance", "If it weren't for _____ I could have what I deserve in life", or "If my spouse treated me better I could feel better about myself". All of these statements indicate a person is looking in places where "the light is better" rather than where the problem really lies.

In a far off distant land many years ago a man was distressed with the amount of nagging that he had to put up with from his wife. Talking to her seemed to go nowhere so he sought out the opinion of the man universally considered to be the wisest man around. He explained his situation to the wise man who briefly considered what he had been told. The wise man then looked confidently at the distressed husband and boldly said, "I have the solution to your problem. Go home this afternoon and invite your mother-in-law to live with you. This is the solution to your problem." Not sure he had just heard the wise man correctly, he asked again, and was again told to move his mother-in-law in with them. He did as he was told, and things actually got worse. Now he had two people in the house who were nagging at him. They took turns and at times worked in tandem with one another. After a week's time the man returned to the wise man to say that things had been even worse than before. He now wanted to know what to do to handle this new situation. The wise man looked up knowingly and said, "Go out to your barn when you get home and move your cow into your home." Certainly the wise man misunderstood what he was asking so he clarified and was given the same instructions. He did so, and now he had two women and a cow constantly making noise at him. After another week's time he goes back to the wise man looking haggard and worn. He gives an update and then asks his advice again. The wise man looks up and tells him, "Go home and move your pig from your barn to the house." Too tired to question, the man does as he is told. He endures another week of even more intense agony. Week after week this scenario repeats itself until the man's barn has been emptied of animals and he is literally on his last nerve. He staggers his way back to the old man, about on the brink of collapse, and the old man puts down his pipe and says the following, "Your house is not fit to live in anymore. Here is what you should do. Go home and put all of your animals back in the barn. Pack up your mother-in-law and move her back to her house. Then go home to sleep in your own bed. Come back first thing in the morning and tell me how things go." The man did as he was told. The next day he returned to the old man, obviously well rested, and proclaimed that peace had been restored in his home and he never so enjoyed spending quiet times with his wife.

This speaks to the fact that everything is relative. Sometimes we get so caught up in the perceived negativity of our situation we forget that things could always be worse. This joke/story makes the point by taking it to the extreme. Quite often, when we take a fair and balanced view of our situation, we do see that while bad things do exist, there is also plenty of good there as well.

It had been a magical day for a young couple. They had exchanged vows and joined their lives as man and wife. They had gone to their hotel room after the reception and were preparing to spend their first night together as a married couple. As the couple disrobed the husband slid off the pants to his tuxedo, smiled at his wife, and tossed the pants to her. She caught them on the fly, and her new husband smiles at her and boldly tells her, "Put these on." The wife quizzically looks at her husband and he again say, with even more bravado, "Put these on." She shrugs her shoulders and begins to slide them over her legs. When she attempts to fasten the pants they slide off of her hips straight to the floor. She attempts a couple of more times with the same results. Frustrated, she says to her husband, "I can't wear these!" To which her husband replies, "That's right. I wear the pants in this family and that is the way it is going to be, understood?" The wife steps out of the pants, slides of her panties, and tosses them to her husband. He catches them and his wife says with the same confidence that he displayed moments earlier, "Put these on." He looks at her like she is crazy and she again states, "Put these on." He complies and is able to get them up to his knees before they will go no further. No matter how hard he tugs they refuse to go any higher. He looks at her and says, "I can't get into these!" His wife smugly replies, "That's right. And as long as you have that attitude, that is the way it's going to be, understood?"

Women like that one. Enough said.

Another young couple from the old west is heading out after their wedding ceremony on their horse-drawn wagon to their new home, a cabin several miles out of town. After a couple of miles on the desolate road the horse rears back for seemingly no reason, stopping the wagon in its tracks. The man quietly gets down from the buckboard, walks in front of the horse, looks the horse right in the eyes, and proclaims, "That's one!" Without saying another word he climbs up on the buckboard and they proceed on down the road. About three miles after the first incident the horse rears back again. The husband climbs down off the buckboard, walks in front of the horse, looks him straight in the eye, and says, "That's two." He climbs back up on the buckboard and they continue down the desolate road. After about five more miles, around the middle of their trip, the horse rears back yet again. The man climbs down off the buckboard, walks in front of the horse, looks the horse straight in the eyes, and says, "That's three." With that he pulled out his pistol and shot the horse dead. The wife witnesses this whole scene unfold before her very eyes. She realizes that they are in the middle of nowhere and her new husband has just eliminated their chance of getting to their destination. She starts yelling at him at the top of her lungs, berating him for being so short-sighted in eliminating their means of transportation. At this her husband climbs back onto the buckboard, turns to his wife, and proclaims, "That's one!"

Men like that one. Enough said.

A guy goes to a psychologist to have some personality testing done. The psychologist says that the first test that they are going to do involves the client to look at a series of ink blots and to describe what he sees in the shapes. The guy acknowledges that he understands and the psychologist proceeds to show him the first picture. The man studies it for a minute and then states, "It's a naked woman." The psychologist, surprised by the response, looks at the ink blot and not seeing anything of the sort, moves onto the next picture. The man looks intently and then says with great confidence, "It's a woman's breast!" Again surprised by the response, the psychologist quizzically looks at the card and proceeds to the next picture. As the third picture is presented, the man looks, cocks his head slightly, and says, "It's two people making love." With this, the psychologist slams down the remaining cards and sternly says to the man, "That is your problem. You are obsessed with sex!" The man calmly looks at the psychologist and says, "Look Doc, you are the one with all the dirty pictures."

Psychologists like that one.

One fine, sunny Saturday a guy was sitting on his couch watching football when his doorbell rang. He got up to see who it was and when he opened the door no one was there. He looked all around, sure that he was not hearing things, and just as he was about to close the door he looked down and saw a snail on his doorstep. Not being a fan of the slimy creatures he picked it up and chucked it as far as he could throw it. He returns to finish watching the game. Two full years go by and he is again watching TV in his living room. The doorbell rings and he gets up to go answer it. He opens the door and no one is there. He looks all around and then looks to the ground where he sees the snail. The snail looks up at him and says, "What the hell was that about?!"

Everybody likes that one.

Lastly, I want to share with you, the reader, a tiny little diagnostic theory that I have been devising. I have to admit, I debated whether to include it for fear of legal reprisal at the hands of the Disney Corporation. But with much consideration, and very little fear that this particular piece of work will ever place Disney in any sort of peril, I decided to include it. It fits well in this section, as we have previously discussed how an individual's personality will be a strong indicator as to what they find humorous. Likewise, I believe that a person's favorite *Winnie the Pooh* character may be predictive of the type of mental health issue a person may be predisposed to develop at some point in their lives. This is based on the fact that each of the characters in the *Winnie the Pooh* series "bear" a striking similarity to several diagnoses in the Diagnostic And Statistical Manual-IV (the diagnostic book used by clinicians to assign diagnoses). Now before you think this theory is the result of too many hours behind the keyboard, hear me out on this one. Let's take a look:

- Piglet-Generalized Anxiety Disorder
- Owl-Narcissistic Personality Disorder
- Rabbit-Obsessive-Compulsive Disorder
- Gopher-Type A Personality, Workaholic
- Kanga & Roo-Mother-Infant Attachment Disorder
- Eeyore-Major Depression
- Tigger-Bipolar I, Manic Phase
- Winnie the Pooh-Mildly Mentally Retarded
- Christopher Robin-Schizophrenia

Kind of puts a different spin on things, doesn't it? Now if I am wrong about the Disney Corporation being upset by this theory and they want to get together with me on a mental health theme park idea, hit me up on Facebook and we'll do lunch!

12
Letter To Me

A couple of months ago, while attending a service at Wheaton Bible Church, I was given the idea that would eventually become the conclusion of this book. Actually, the idea originated sometime before, but it really came into view on this day. The minister was Jeff Walser, and he was talking about something that he had done recently at the request of his son. His son asked him to write a letter to himself when he was eighteen. I listened intently as Jeff detailed many of the lessons in his life that he had learned, and was in the process of retrospectively previewing what is to come in the life of this young man. Coincidently, the country artist Brad Paisley has a song entitled *Letter To Me*, in which he passes along some words of wisdom to himself at an earlier time in his life. Well, when such a theme keeps circling the airport of your life you sooner or later take notice. The following will be my attempt at this endeavor:

Dear Herb,

As I sit here writing this to you I am struck with the emotion that wells in me. Nostalgia grips me as I look back on what you have to look forward to in your life. The first thing I want to tell you is that you are in for one heck of a ride. You will meet people and have experiences that will blow you away. There will be much more good than bad, but make sure you pay attention to all of it, because it all goes into who you will become.

First of all, don't be so unsure of yourself. You and I both know that you always question yourself and are unsure if you are good enough (whatever that means). This will be a problem for you early on, and it will cause you to miss out on some nice opportunities. You are a fairly smart guy, not the smartest of the smart, but certainly not the dumbest of the dumb. Trust yourself because other people's thoughts and ideas are not necessarily better than your own. Those nice things that people say to you are not out of obligation, they are telling you what they really think and feel. It will take you a while to truly understand the courage that dwells in you, but it will always be there for you.

People . . . you will meet a lot of people in your life. Most of them will be really good people, and some, not so much, but they will all have an impact on you. Some of them will be in your life for a short period of time, some will come and go, and some will be there for the duration. It will be harder for you to learn to receive in relationships than for you to give; you will have to learn that when you accept kindness from others you actually afford them the gift of giving to others. Mean people suck, and you will always have a problem with them. Try to approach them with understanding, but don't tolerate their behavior too long. There will be times when you are sort of mean yourself, or at least insensitive to others. It doesn't happen very often, but when it does, recognize it, take responsibility for your actions, and try to learn from it. Also, make sure that you forgive yourself when you fall short. You will struggle with this from time to time.

Work . . . You will work a lot in your life. You will often struggle with whether this is a necessity for you or whether you work too much out of fear. Enjoy your work, but make sure you have balance in your life. Your work will be rewarding for you, but there will be times when you are lost and unsure. Those times will help you grow as an individual. Taking time for fun will be a challenge for you, and don't be so serious all the time.

Family . . . don't wait too long to figure out that you are blessed with an awesome family. For longer than you think, you will remember fondly your Aunt Nancy calling you "Derb" and your Aunt Gloria saying, "So long, be nice, and watch for cars". Your parents are amazing people. You think you know that now, but you don't know the half of it. They will always be there for you, especially in your darkest moments. You will rarely know comfort like the comfort you feel when you hear them say that, "it will be OK". Your dad will teach you a lot. Growing up it was sort of intimidating to be around him, not because that was how he wanted you to feel, but because he was just so good at everything he did. You will see that you gained a lot from being with him because he really believes in you. Also, don't wait until he has his accident to tell him you love him. You avoid that out of fear, and you should never let fear control your life like that, and skipping opportunities to let someone know how you feel will never turn out well. Your mom will never stop trying to be your mommie. That is not about you, but rather because she loves that role so much, and she is darn good at it. Let her enjoy that, and don't give her such a hard time about it. She is a great cook, a great mender of hearts, and she will teach you a lot about the importance of family. Make sure you spend as much time with grandma as you can because she will be gone way too soon in your life. She is a strong woman even if she doesn't stand over five feet tall. Make sure you understand the love that you feel when you look in her eyes because it is true love. Your grandfather will play a lot bigger role in your life than you would think. You were named after him, and it will be worth all of the teasing that you took growing up with the name Herb. The legend of who he was will inspire you to try to develop those qualities in yourself. Your siblings, Chris, Jim, and Amy, are really special people, too. They will be one of the constants that will be there throughout your life. Try to make sure that you spend more time with them. Making time for important things in your life will be something you struggle with often.

Relationships . . . you will have quite a ride when it comes to relationships. I know that you feel like you have this one figured out right now, but you don't. There will be many twists and turns in this part of your life. Some of your relationships will fail. These will be the lowest points in your life, and you will question whether you can, or even want to, go on. You will be hurt and angry about this. Don't allow yourself to be down about this any longer than you have to be. Eventually, you will move on and be able to see the good in these without it being contaminated with the bad. Resentment is a toxic agent that will work to erode your soul. Out of one of these relationships will come two of the most precious things in the world to you, your children, Amanda and Jonathon. Don't ever lose sight of the importance of spending time with them. They will grow up all too quickly, and you will miss the times when they were small. Appreciate who they are as individuals, and it is your job to connect with them. They will not be near you as much as you had planned, so you will have to work at it. You will find that it is well worth the effort. You will teach them many things, but in the end it is they who will teach you more, so pay attention. You will eventually have a wonderful woman named Pat in your life. She will challenge you to step outside of the familiar, so don't fight it so much. She will always remind you to have fun, something you are not so good at reminding yourself. She will also bring with her two terrific children of her own, Elise and Andy. Again, remember that it is your job to create a history with them. It's challenging, but the rewards you will gain are more than worth the investment. You will always have to work on balancing work and family. In these times, don't forget to remember your priorities and values.

The last thing that I want to share with you is in many ways your most important struggle; it's your relationship with God. Throughout much of your life, God will be a mystery to you. There will even be times when you question His existence. There will be times when you fake the relationship just to appease others, but in your heart you will know this is not right. Much of your difficulties with this relationship will be around control, or at least the illusion of control. Over the next few years, fear will play a role in your life, even though you will not be aware of it at the time. You will tell yourself that you have to have all the answers to issues that arise in your life. In a lot of ways, nothing could be further from the truth. In reality, you are just afraid of what might happen if you don't believe that you have all the answers. It won't be until a painful divorce followed by the geographic separation from your children, that you will be broken enough to see the truth. That moment will happen at the intersection of Reed Road and Rt 129 in Braidwood, IL. That is when you will put down the burden of having to have all the answers yourself, and realize that you just have to turn towards someone who does. You will not understand the idea of "fearing God" until you understand that it really means respecting Him. You will also understand that even though He had to wait for you to turn to Him, He did not wait for this time to bestow blessings upon your life. He has always had good things in store for you. He will always put just the right person in your life at just the right time. He will understand when you fall short (and believe me you will). Most important of all, He will never stop loving you.

In conclusion, remember this about the years to come in your life: Your mistakes will make you smarter; your hurts will make you stronger; your fears will get you to pay attention; and your dreams will give you direction. Great things lie ahead of you, make sure you take time to enjoy the ride.

Herb

Post Note

I realized after I read through the rough draft of this work that I had neglected to include a story that I love to tell that really captures the main points put forth in this book. Many years ago I was a member of an adult Sunday School class at a church I was attending in Wilmington, IL. The class was filled with individuals who possessed a treasure trove of wisdom. Eventually I became the class facilitator, but truth be told, I always felt like I learned much more than I ever taught. One of the ladies in the class was a woman by the name of Virginia Weaver. Virginia was a woman who had a real presence about her. She always carried herself with grace and dignity. She was a widow and had taught at the local elementary school for many years.

One Sunday in class we were talking about the subject of beliefs and the power of thought to influence not only our experience of the world, but also our ability to function in it. Virginia stated that when she was in her early sixties she told her husband that she wanted to learn how to ride a bike. She had grown up rather poor and her family could not afford the expense of a bike so she had never learned to ride. Her husband went right out and bought her a very nice bike and installed training wheels to help her keep the bike up while she learned to ride. Virginia loved the bike and used it to ride around the neighborhood visiting friends to garden or to just have tea. One day, several months into her bike-riding career, Virginia rode her bike to a friend's house down the block and after a lovely visit she walked to the drive to get on her bike and ride home. When her friend saw the bike she exclaimed, "Look at those training wheels. Why, they are bent so far up they don't even touch the ground anymore." At the moment of this realization Virginia was panic-stricken. She believed that she could only ride the bike with the security of the training wheels. And despite the fact that she had ridden it over to her friend's house in the exact same condition in which it now sat, she did not believe that she could ride it. She ended up walking her bike home and parking it in the garage for several days.

After a few days of reflecting on this situation, Virginia finally convinced herself to embrace the facts. She could ride the bike without the training wheels as evidenced by the fact that she had actually been doing that (unknowingly) for several weeks. She went out to the garage, took out her bike, climbed on board and resumed the bike rides that she had grown to love before she allowed her fear to rob her of it. She accessed her courage, overcame her fear, and freed herself to enjoy rides on her bike and visits with friends.

Thank you for taking the time to share in some of my stories and theories on life. I hope that you found the time spent to be valuable, entertaining, and perhaps even educational. By accessing your courage, controlling only what you can control in life, and cleaning out that which has exceeded its usefulness, I hope that you are able to define for yourself a life that provides happiness and meaning for now and the years to come.

References

Amen, Daniel G. *Change Your Brain Change Your Life,* Three Rivers Press, New York, NY 1998.

Chapman, Gary. *The Five Love Languages,* Northfield Publishing, Chicago, IL 1995.

Eggerichs, Emerson. *Love & Respect,* Thomas Nelson Publishers, Nashville, TN 2004.

Gottman, John M. *The Seven Principles For Making Marriage Work,* Crown Publishers, New York, NY 1999.

Kubler Ross, Elizabeth. *On Death And Dying,* Simon & Schuster/Collier Books 1970

Richo, David. *How To Be An Adult In Relationships,* Shambala Publishing, Boston, MA 2002.

Smalley, Gary. *If Only He Knew,* Zondervan Publishing House, Grand Rapids, MI 1979.

Smalley, Gary with John Trent. *Love Is A Decision.* Word Publishing, Dallas, TX 1989.

Smalley, Gary. *Secrets To Lasting Love,* Simon & Shuster, New York, NY 2000

Ziglar, Zig. *Courtship After Marriage,* Oliver-Nelson Books, Nashville, TN 1990